THE OLD TESTAMENT WORLD

THE PEOPLE
AND THE PROMISE

by
LAURENCE N. FIELD

Illustrated by Lee Mero

Issued under auspices of the
Board of Parish Education of
The American Lutheran Church

Augsburg Publishing House, Minneapolis 15, Minn.

THE PEOPLE AND THE PROMISE
a reprint of
Family Bible Story Book (Old Testament)
Copyright © Augsburg Publishing House 1957
Library of Congress Catalog Card No. 57-7959

MANUFACTURED IN THE UNITED STATES OF AMERICA

FOREWORD

The most rememberable form of information is a story which captures events in sequence, teachings in a setting, and people in relationship with other people in the situation. What God did and how people responded is a great and dramatic message recorded for us in the pages of Holy Scripture. The record of the drama of God and men—a drama in which you and I are playing a part right now—is worth studying in every way we can imagine. One of those ways includes reading the essential story of each episode, each character.

This reading book provides a ready source for getting the basic message in story form. It brings us the consistency of one man's point of view—something like a father relaying ancient truths to his children, or a guide pointing out the main features to be noted by the people in his party. In swiftly moving chapters that tie together many threads of information and of interpretation, Dr. Laurence Field retells the basic story of *The People and the Promise*. This reading book can help you grasp the central emphasis and think through a summary of each period or person in the great drama of Old Testament events.

The tone of this retelling is reverent; we are always aware of the presence of God. The purpose of the story is personal; it has to do with us. You will find it interesting. You may even want to read the whole story at a sitting rather than waiting to see it unfold piecemeal through a longer course of study.

This reading book is meant to help you with your study of the Bible, not to take the place of reading The Book itself. Use this reading book along with the Bible, with the guidance of the workbook, and with special projects of research and report: you will gain a grasp of the absorbing story of

The People and the Promise. You may even catch on that you, though living in a later time, are one of *the people,* and that *the promise* is to *you.*

The careful research behind Lee Mero's pictorial presentations can give to you a better understanding of the times and places in which the Old Testament scenes were set. These pictures, charts, and maps will serve you as a kind of built-in Bible dictionary. They may also suggest to you fascinating further explorations which you may wish to make with more detailed resources.

C. RICHARD EVENSON

CONTENTS

I INTRODUCTION
PAGE
1. The Book 3
2. The Land 7

II CREATION TO THE TOWER OF BABEL
3. The Creation 14
4. The Fall 19
5. The Flood and the Tower of Babel 23

III THE PATRIARCHS
6. Abraham, Father of the Faithful 32
7. The Terrible End of Sodom and Gomorrah 36
8. Isaac 39
9. Jacob and Esau 44
10. Jacob Leaves Home 47

IV EGYPT
11. Joseph 54
12. From Prison to Palace 59
13. Reunion in Egypt 63

V BIRTH OF A NATION
14. Birth and Training of Moses 68
15. Moses' Call and the Contest with Pharaoh 73
16. The Red Sea and Sinai 77
17. The Giving of the Law 82
18. The Death of Moses 86
19. The Conquest of Canaan 89

VI A STRUGGLING KINGDOM
20. The Judges 96
21. Ruth 100
22. The Last of the Judges 105
23. King Saul 109
24. Death of Saul 114

VII ISRAEL'S GOLDEN AGE
25. King David 120
26. King Solomon 124

VIII A DIVIDED KINGDOM
27. The Kingdom Divided 132
28. Elijah 136
29. Elisha—End of the Northern Kingdom 140
30. Kings and Prophets of Judah 145
31. End of the Southern Kingdom 150

IX EXILE AND POST-EXILE
32. The Babylonian Captivity 156
33. End of the Babylonian Captivity 160
34. The Maccabees 164
35. End of the Old Testament 168
36. Rome and the Fullness of Time 172

THE PEOPLE AND THE PROMISE

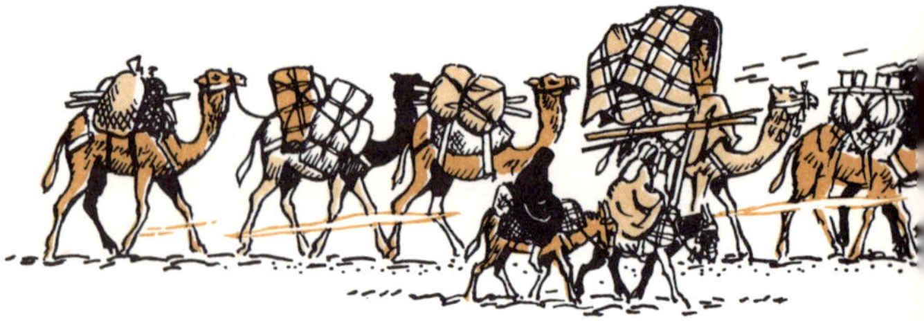

I
INTRODUCTION

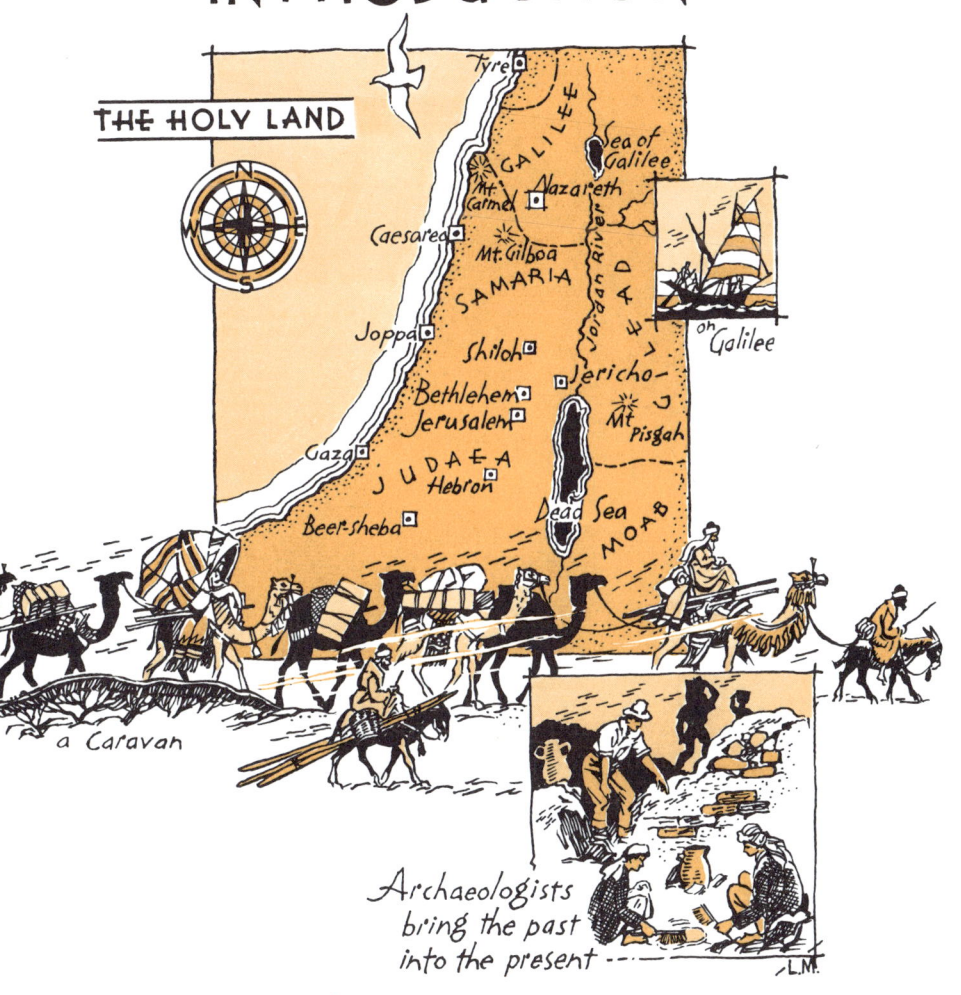

THE HOLY LAND

a Caravan

Archaeologists bring the past into the present --

CHAPTER ONE

THE BOOK

The most important book in the world is the Bible. It has been reprinted more times and in more languages that any other book. Thousands have risked their lives and even died to preserve it and its message and to make it available to others, and thousands stand ready to do so again if need should arise. What a wonderful Book it is! The Bible is God's own Word, from Himself to man. In it He tells how the world came to be, and that it was a good world, ruled by love. Then sin came in and spoiled everything. But God's love did not cease. In the fulness of time He sent His Son, Jesus Christ, to pay the penalty for sin and assure mankind of forgiveness. Christ died and arose again in victory over death, so that we, too, may have eternal life through Him. And to give us assurance of these things and power to be and remain His children, He sent His Holy Spirit to be our Guide and Strength. This is the basis of our Christian faith. Truly then, the Bible is the Book of Life. No wonder that it is so important and precious!

As we pick it up, we note its size. It is a large book because it covers such a great length of time and has so much to tell. But it can be shortened and still keep its wonderful message. For instance, many people carry with them an edition so small that it can be slipped into one's purse or pocket. It contains only the New Testament and the Psalms, but the Bible's central message is still complete. If we had to, we could take only one of its many Books, the Gospel of John, and have the story of Salvation intact. And if we had to limit ourselves still more, we could tear out all but one page or chapter, the third chapter of John, and still have the core of God's Word. Indeed, if we lost all but one single verse, namely John 3:16, we would have a miniature Bible and could be saved by it. It is indeed a wonderful Book!

> FOR GOD SO LOVED THE WORLD, THAT HE GAVE HIS ONLY BEGOTTEN SON, THAT WHOSOEVER BELIEVETH IN HIM SHOULD NOT PERISH, BUT HAVE EVERLASTING LIFE. John 3:16

The Bible is really sixty-six books in one. It took many different writers more than fifteen hundred years to complete them all. It is divided into two main parts, the Old Testament and the New, and the Old Testament is several times as long as the New. It covers all the period before Christ ("B.C."), or more accurately from Creation to about 400 B.C. The Old Testament contains thirty-nine Books, varying in length from one chapter (Obadiah), to sixty-six (Isaiah) and a hundred and fifty (the book of Psalms). It was written in the Hebrew language, but with a few chapters and phrases from other ancient languages. Between the Old Testament and the New there is a gap of several centuries, just as though the Old were waiting for the New. The New Testament covers the times of Christ and the Apostles ("A.D."), and on in prophecy until the end of the world. It totals twenty-seven books, many of them very short; and was written in Greek, the ancient language of culture, with a few phrases from other languages such as Latin, Hebrew, and Aramaic. Thus we see that the Bible covers all history, in fact or in prophecy, from eternity to eternity. At the center is Jesus, God and Man, in whom time and eternity, and earth and heaven meet.

Let us memorize the books of the Bible and learn to locate them. We ought to be so at home among them that we can find any book or passage quickly and easily.

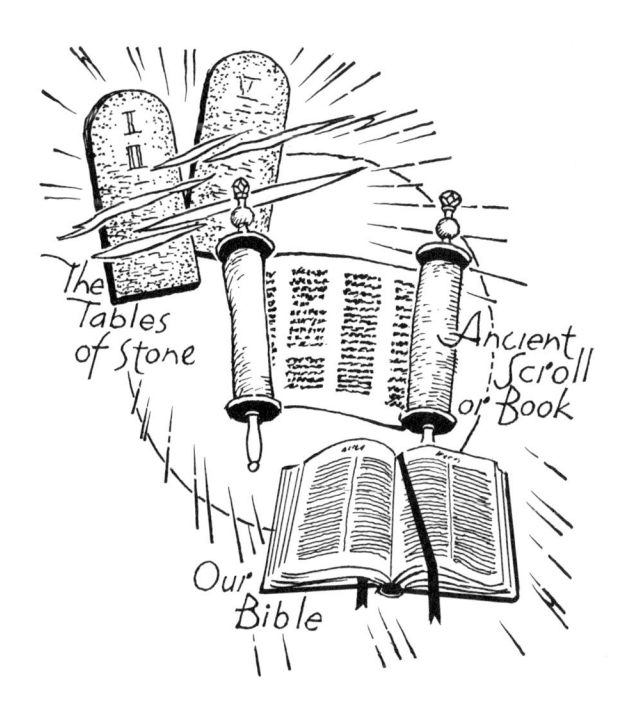

THE OLD TESTAMENT (39 Books)

The Five Books of Moses, Called the Pentateuch
Genesis   Exodus   Leviticus   Numbers   Deuteronomy

The Twelve Historical Books
Joshua   I and II Samuel   Ezra
Judges   I and II Kings   Nehemiah
Ruth   I and II Chronicles   Esther

The Five Poetical Books
Job   Psalms   Proverbs   Ecclesiastes   Song of Solomon

The Five Major Prophets
Isaiah   Jeremiah   Lamentations   Ezekiel   Daniel

The Twelve Minor Prophets
Hosea   Jonah   Zephaniah
Joel   Micah   Haggai
Amos   Nahum   Zechariah
Obadiah   Habakkuk   Malachi

THE NEW TESTAMENT (27 Books)

The Four Gospels
Matthew   Mark   Luke   John

The One Book of History
The Book of Acts

The Epistles
Romans   Colossians   Hebrews
I and II Corinthians   I and II Thessalonians   James
Galatians   I and II Timothy   I and II Peter
Ephesians   Titus   I, II and III John
Philippians   Philemon   Jude

The One Book of Prophecy
The Book of Revelation

CHAPTER TWO

THE LAND

The Bible was born in the land of Palestine. The Holy Land, as it is called, is very small, a mere dot among the nations. It lies at the eastern end of the Mediterranean Sea, with Africa to the southwest, Europe to the northwest, and all Asia to the rear. But in ancient days it was the strategic center of the land mass of civilization, and was the crossroads of the nations. It was no idle boast of the Jews that their fatherland was the center of the universe. Highways and caravan routes from all corners of the commercial world crossed and criss-crossed Palestine all down the ages, both before and after the days of Christ, and many of these highways are still in constant use. In a military sense also, Palestine was the crossroads of the world, but in a grim sense, for it lay as a sort of buffer state between world powers; and here their armies often met and fought, for they had to cross Palestine to get at each other. Poor little Palestine was at times at her wit's end trying to decide which side to follow in order to survive.

The Holy Land lies about as far south as northern Florida and Georgia, and has almost a sub-tropical climate, depending on altitude and nearness to the sea. Its rainfall varies, and did so most distressingly at times to the ancients. In good years it could really be a land "flowing with milk and honey," while in bad years there could be absolute want. The Hebrews learned very directly to look to God for weather, food, and security.

A glance at the map will show that a river, a lake, and a city dominate the land. Each one is most unusual and interesting. The Jordan river rises about seventeen hundred feet above sea level, and after a distance of about a hundred and thirty-five miles empties into a lake twelve hundred and ninety feet below sea level. The river is very crooked, and to cover that distance it actually flows twice that far. Way down to our own times no commercial vessels have ever navigated its waters and no important city has ever flourished on its banks. It rises in a cave, flows through a gorge in the midst of wilderness, and empties into a lake that knows no outlet. Yet it is one of the most famous rivers of history. The valley of the Jordan is almost a thousand feet lower than any other part of the earth's surface not covered by water.

The Dead Sea, into which it empties, is even more interesting. Almost fifty miles long, by some ten miles wide, it lies in a tremendous hollow of the earth that seems to be without parallel for depth. Its surface is almost thirteen hundred feet below sea level, while its bottom at the northeast is thirteen hundred feet below that again. At the south it is very shallow. There being no lower place to which its water can flow, it has no known outlet; nevertheless evaporation is so rapid that the water level remains constant. The Dead Sea contains more salts and minerals in solution than the ocean itself, nearly twenty-six percent. No fish or organic life thrives in its waters; no boats plow its surface; and no cities are on its banks. It is indeed the DEAD Sea.

A much smaller lake claims the attention of Bible students, and that only because of ONE MAN who graced its neighborhood with His presence. In the Old Testament, this lake plays no role whatsoever. Not until Jesus of Nazareth came, did it become immortal. It is the Sea of Galilee.

fishermen of Galilee

Jerusalem is one of the oldest cities on earth. It is still the spiritual capital of the world, and is that for two major religions beside our own. It has been destroyed and rebuilt so many times that it would be difficult to count them all. But it has survived every one of its enemies, until its very name has become the name of that final city "built without hands," which God has promised in the last great "fulness of time," namely the New Jerusalem, which is Heaven.

Our own times have seen an amazing upsurge in knowledge of Bible times and events and people, through the discoveries and painstaking scholarship of archaeologists. It is as though God Almighty has made use of the very destructiveness that converted the Holy Land into a series of outlived cities and rubble filled mounds and ruins, so that they might keep their secrets intact until the science and devotion of our own day could unravel them. Never have knowledge and understanding of the Land and the Book been so intimate and complete as right now. Even the caves of Palestine are yielding a harvest of precious manuscripts, such as the Dead Sea Scrolls, helping to establish with certainty the age and reliability of the Book of Books. And more awaits the spade of the excavator.

Such is that little corner of the globe where God revealed Himself as in no other place, and where there took place so many events loaded with importance for our spiritual and eternal welfare.

II
FROM THE CREATION TO THE TOWER OF BABEL

"The birds of the air"

"...an ark of gopher wood"
Gen. 6:14

"And the Lord God planted a garden"
Gen 2:8

"The fish of the sea"

"In the beginning God!"

CHAPTER THREE

THE CREATION

The first chapter of the Bible tells about the creation of the world and everything in it, including human beings. The account is poetic and is very short and simple, only about six hundred words. It is therefore not to be expected that with such tremendous subject matter, every detail should be covered; there are indeed many questions that one would like to ask. Godly science has added much to the understanding of the opening chapter of Genesis, but we shall doubtless never understand the full glory of the Creation story until we have graduated from this world and are together with God in Heaven.

Meanwhile, how beautiful and simple and orderly is the Lord's own account of Creation. "In the beginning, God!" No wisdom can get farther than that. "In the beginning, God created the heavens and the earth. . . . And the spirit of God was moving over the face of the waters. . . . And God said: Let there be light. And there was light. . . . And God called the light Day, and the darkness he called Night. And there was evening and there was morning one day. . . . And God made the firmament and separated the waters which were under the firmament from the waters which were above the firmament. And it was so. And God called the firmament Heaven. . . . And God said: Let the waters under the heavens be gathered together into one place and let the dry land appear. And God called the dry land Earth, and the waters that were gathered together He called Seas. And God saw that it was good. . . . And God said: Let the earth put forth vegetation, plants yielding seed, and fruit trees bearing fruit in which is their seed, each according to its kind, upon the earth. And it was so. . . . And God said: Let there be lights in the firmament of the heavens and to separate the day from the night; and let them be for signs and for seasons and for days and years, and let them be lights in the firmament of the heavens to give light upon the earth. And it was so. And God made the two great lights, the greater light to rule the day, and the lesser light to rule the night; he made the stars also. . . . And God said: Let the waters bring forth swarms of living creatures, and let birds fly above the earth across the firmament of the heavens. So God created the great sea monsters and every living creature that moves, with which the waters swarm, according to their kinds, and every winged bird according to its kind. And God saw that it was good. And God blessed them, saying: Be fruitful and multiply and fill the waters in the seas, and let birds multiply on the earth. . . . And God said: Let the

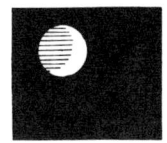

earth bring forth living creatures according to their kinds: cattle and creeping things and beasts of the earth according to their kind. And it was so.

"Then God said: Let us make man in our image, after our likeness; and let them have dominion over the flesh of the sea and over the birds of the air and over the cattle and over all the earth, and over every creeping thing that creeps upon the earth. So God created man in his own image, in the image of God he created him; male and female he created them. And God blessed them, and God said to them: Be fruitful and multiply, and fill the earth and subdue it; and have dominion over the fish of the sea and over the birds of the air and over every living thing that moves upon the earth. And God said: Behold, I have given you every plant yielding seed which is upon the face of all the earth, and every tree with seed in its fruit; you shall have them for food. . . . And it was so. And God saw everything that he had made, and behold it was very good. And there was evening and there was morning a sixth day.

"Thus the heavens and the earth were finished and all the host of them. And on the seventh day God finished his work which he had done, and he rested on the seventh day from all his work which he had done. So God blessed the seventh day and hallowed it, because on it God rested from all his work which he had done in creation.

"The Lord God formed man of dust from the ground, and breathed into his nostrils the breath of life; and man became a living being. . . . And the Lord planted a garden in Eden, in the east, and there he put the man whom he had formed." It was fitting that our first forefather should be called Adam, for the name means Ground or Earth. But Adam became lonesome for a helpmeet, especially when he noticed that all of God's creatures had mates. "Then the Lord said: It is not good that man should be alone; I will make him a helper fit for him. . . . So the Lord caused a deep sleep to fall upon the man, and while he slept took one of his ribs and closed up its place with flesh; and the rib which the Lord God had taken from the man he made into a woman and brought her to the man. Then the man said: This at last is bone of my bones and flesh of my flesh; she shall be called Woman because she was taken out of man. Therefore a man leaves his father and his mother and cleaves to his wife, and they become one flesh. And the man and his wife were both naked, and were not ashamed."

With poetic charm and dignity the Bible tells the story of the creation of man and woman, and of the institution of marriage and the first home in the Garden of Eden, or Paradise. Adam called his wife Eve, "because she was the mother of all living."

Genesis 1 and 2

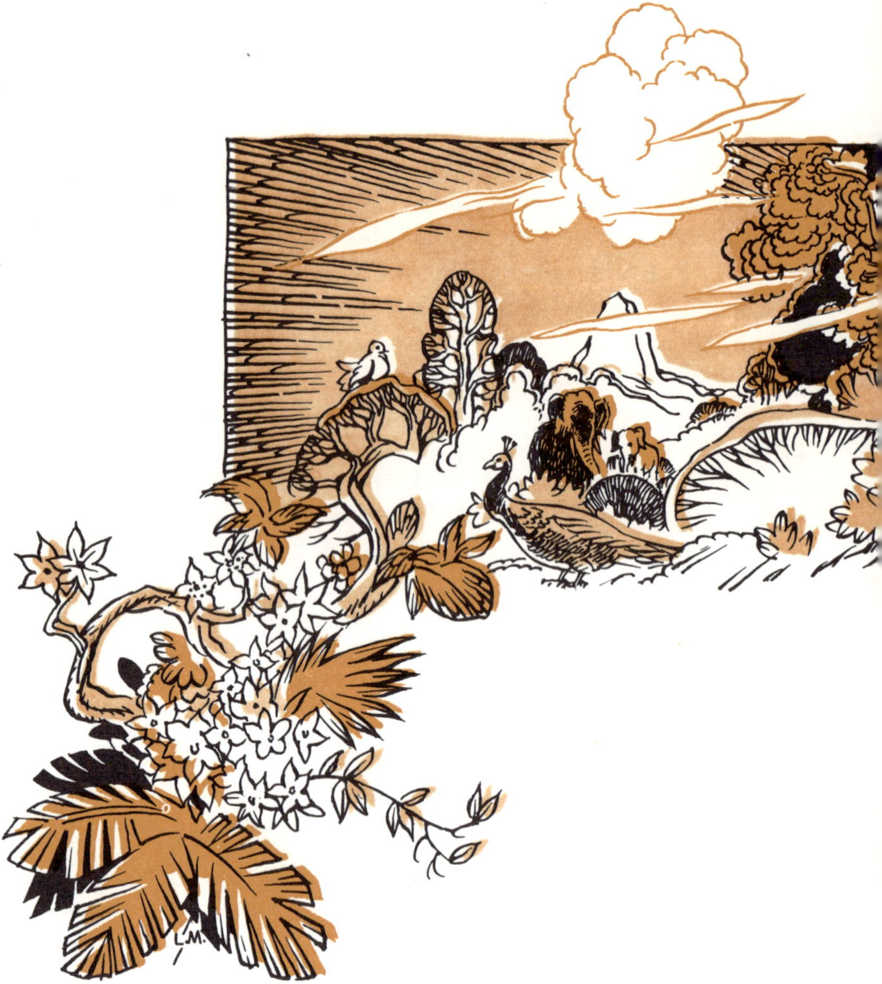
L.M.

CHAPTER FOUR

THE FALL

Eden was a place of great freedom, because it was sinless and was ruled by love. But as a test of obedience, God laid down one simple law for Adam and Eve. At the center of the Garden there were two very special trees, one the Tree of Life and the other the Tree of Knowledge of Good and Evil. The Bible does not explain them completely. Concerning the Tree of Knowledge of Good and Evil, God simply said: "You shall not eat of its fruit, neither shall you touch it, lest you die." But Satan, the Evil One, was very cunning. In the guise of a serpent, he tempted Eve, to her ruin, and introduced sin into the world. "Did God say that you should not eat of any of the trees in the Garden?" he asked her. She explained that it was only the Tree of Knowledge of Good and Evil. The serpent replied: "You will not die. God knows that when you eat of it, your eyes will be opened and you will be like God, knowing good and evil." And Eve, looking at the tree, saw that it was good for food and that it was a delight to the eyes and that the tree was to be desired to make one wise. So she took and ate some fruit and gave some also to her husband.

Now their eyes were indeed opened and they became aware of sin. With it there came also the sense of guilt, shame, and fear. Since the charm of innocence was now gone, they saw that they were naked and sewed together aprons or loin cloths of leaves. And being now afraid of God, they tried to hide from Him. When evening came, He called to them: "Adam, where are you?" Then they had to stand before Him in their guilty shame. Adam tried to blame Eve, and she tried to blame the serpent; but all were guilty and had to receive judgment. To the serpent, God said: "Cursed are you among all creatures! Upon your belly you shall go, and dust shall you eat all the days of your life." To Eve, He said: "I will greatly multiply your pain in childbearing; yet your desire shall be for your husband, and he shall rule over you." And to Adam, He said: "Cursed is the ground because of you. Thorns and thistles it shall bring forth to you. In the sweat of your face you shall eat bread till you return to the ground, for out of it you were taken; you are dust, and to dust you shall return."

Now they had to leave their home in Paradise and move out into a hostile world. The Tree of Life, too, was taken away, and an angel with a sword guarded the way back. But this was not the worst. Their sinfulness had to be passed on to all who came after them. "Therefore as sin came into the world through one man and death through sin, so death spread to all men because all men sinned" (Romans 5:12). This dreadful tendency to evil, with which all people are born, is called Original Sin. But even in His judgment God's love shone through. To His words to the serpent He added a prophecy and a promise: "I will put enmity between you and the woman, and between your seed and her seed; he shall bruise your head and you shall bruise his heel." This has come down as the first prophecy of the coming of the Savior. In our Old Testament studies we shall find many more.

The terrible story of sin and its consequences had just begun.

Adam and Eve's first son became a murderer, and his brother became the victim. Cain was tiller of the ground, while Abel kept sheep. When the two brothers brought their offerings to the Lord, Abel received the blessing ahead of Cain, because he crowned his with love, while his brother did not. Cain's heart became filled with hatred. God warned him, and at the same time encouraged him to mend his ways so that he too could be blest. But Cain would not. One day he invited Abel out into the field, and there he killed him. "Where is your brother?" the Lord asked him. Sullenly he replied: "I do not know; am I my brother's keeper?" God said: "The voice of your brother's blood is crying to me from the ground. And now you are cursed; you shall be a fugitive and a wanderer." Humbled and frightened, Cain replied: "My punishment is greater than I can bear." God put a brand on him so that people would recognize the murderer and keep away from him; but they were not permitted to take revenge on him. So in this judgment, too, God left a reminder of divine mercy. Cain however remained an evil man, as did his descendants after him. But they were cunning. As time went on, they built cities and became rich; they also invented tools, especially of destruction. Polygamy is first mentioned in connection with Cain's descendants.

But there were good people too. In place of Abel, God gave Adam and Eve another son whom they named Seth. He and his children loved the Lord and kept alive the golden promise of a Messiah to come, who would redeem men from their sins. One of the most lovable men of this period was Enoch. Both the Old and the New Testaments praise him and tell how he did not have to die like other people, but was "translated" in a miraculous way. In those times when the world was young, people lived much longer than they have since then. Enoch lived three hundred and sixty-five years. But that did not compare with his father, who lived to be nine hundred and sixty-two, nor with his son Methuselah who lived longer than any other person, nine hundred and sixty-nine. Adam reached nine hundred and thirty years, and Seth nine hundred and twelve. Yes, there were good people too, but the wicked ones crowded them out or polluted them until the whole world became wicked.

Genesis 3-5

ENOCH WALKED WITH GOD
Gen. 5:24

CHAPTER FIVE

THE FLOOD AND THE TOWER OF BABEL

After the fall of man, the generations that followed became more and more evil. When we come to the time of Noah, we find that only he and his family were left of those who loved God and lived decent lives. God therefore decided to destroy everything and begin over again. But Noah and his household were spared. He was instructed to build a great ship or Ark, so that his family could be preserved in the flood that was coming, and with them representative animals of the various species, so that they could replenish the animal kingdom again. It took a long time to build the Ark. Meanwhile God used it as an object lesson, and Noah preached and warned the people many times of their impending doom. But they would not listen. Finally the terrible storm and flood broke, and destruction came upon all of them. Noah and his wife and their three sons and their wives were safely preserved in the Ark, and with them their carefully selected cargo of animals. For a whole year they lived on the boat, until the flood subsided and there was dry land again.

After the deluge, Noah gratefully built an altar and offered a sacrifice in gratitude for their preservation. Then God gave him and his descendants new instructions, similar to those given to Adam before him. And He made a pledge to Noah and to all mankind after him that He would never again destroy the world with water. The rainbow became the sign and pledge of this promise; and ever since, after storms and behind waterfalls, it has been the symbol of hope and of God's mercy. Noah now became a sort of second Adam or starting point for the human race. His three sons, Shem, Ham, and Japheth, were the ancestors of the three great races of man: the Semites or Asiatics (yellow race), the Hamites or Africans (black race), and the Japhethites or Europeans (white race). Once more God urged mankind to multiply and spread out and take over the whole earth. But there was no move to do so. Instead, the people remained together in the great and fertile plain of Shinar. They never forgot the terrible flood that destroyed their forefathers; but they did forget, or ignored, its lessons, and they defied God

Noah gives thanks

again and became more and more wicked. "Come!" they said, "Let us build ourselves a city and a tower with its top in the heavens; and let us make a name for ourselves, lest we be scattered abroad upon the face of the earth." God was very displeased with their wickedness and defiance, and determined that they should be made to separate and spread out over the earth whether they wanted to or not.

The building of their capital city and the great tower that was to crown it, took a long time, because they had only handmade bricks, with bitumen for mortar; there was no time-saving machinery in those days, such as we have. At this time there was still but one language among men. As time went on, God confused their dialects and set up dissensions between groups, so that they drew more and more apart. Thus the whole venture broke up, each clan or group moving off by itself. So the great unfinished tower became only a monument to their folly, and was given the name "Babel," which means "Confusion." As more time went on, the descendants of Shem tended to move on eastward throughout Asia; the Hamites wandered south and southwest into Africa; and the Japhethites went westward and northwest into Europe. Thus God's command to scatter abroad and take over all of the earth, and not just one corner of it, was fulfilled after all. Meanwhile long ages came and went. The Bible only hints at some of the nations and civilizations that sprang up and flourished and waned again during these prehistoric times. But many of their ruins still remain, and learned and patient men of science and devotion are now busy unearthing and deciphering them. Some day we may know a great deal more about these forgotten races and their history than we do now.

The kingdom of God's children was preserved, but it was well nigh blotted out. Even the Bible is very meager in its revelation of what took place during those centuries. Then God once more started over again. This time He chose a man named Abram, called him away from his place and people, and isolated him so that he could become the forefather of a special nation which He also isolated. God did this so that godliness and the true faith and the precious promise of the Messiah Savior might be preserved. Abram became Abraham, the Father of the Faithful, and we now come to a new great era in the story of the Bible.

Genesis 6-8 and 11

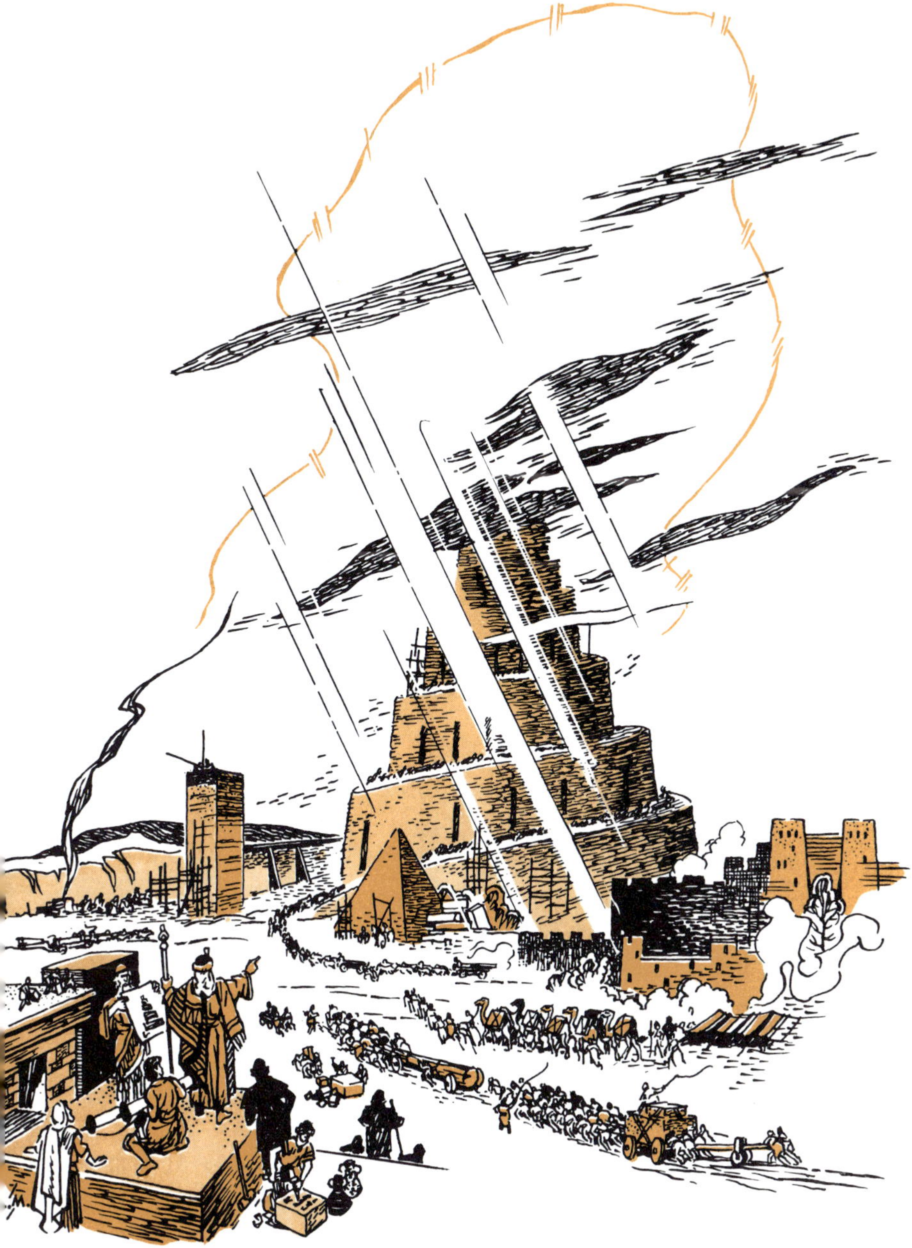

EXAMPLES OF BABYLONIAN-ASSYRIAN ORNAMENTS

The illustrations on these two pages will give an idea of the Babylonian-Assyrian background from which Abraham came.

Excavations during recent years have brought to light fragments and relics of sculpture and engravings on hard stone and terra cotta. These indicate the skill and artistic instinct of this early civilization. Representations of musical instruments imply also that the art of music was not altogether unknown to them.

Some of the relics which have been found date as far back as the time of Abraham, about 2000 B.C. However, the height of Babylonian-Assyrian art seems to have been reached in the period from 800-600 B.C. Elaborate decorations from the palaces of Nebuchadnezzar have been unearthed.

Babylonian-Assyrian art seems to have had a deep influence on Indian, Chinese, Persian and other artists of the east, and students of modern design also find inspiration in the artistic achievements of these people who lived so very long ago.

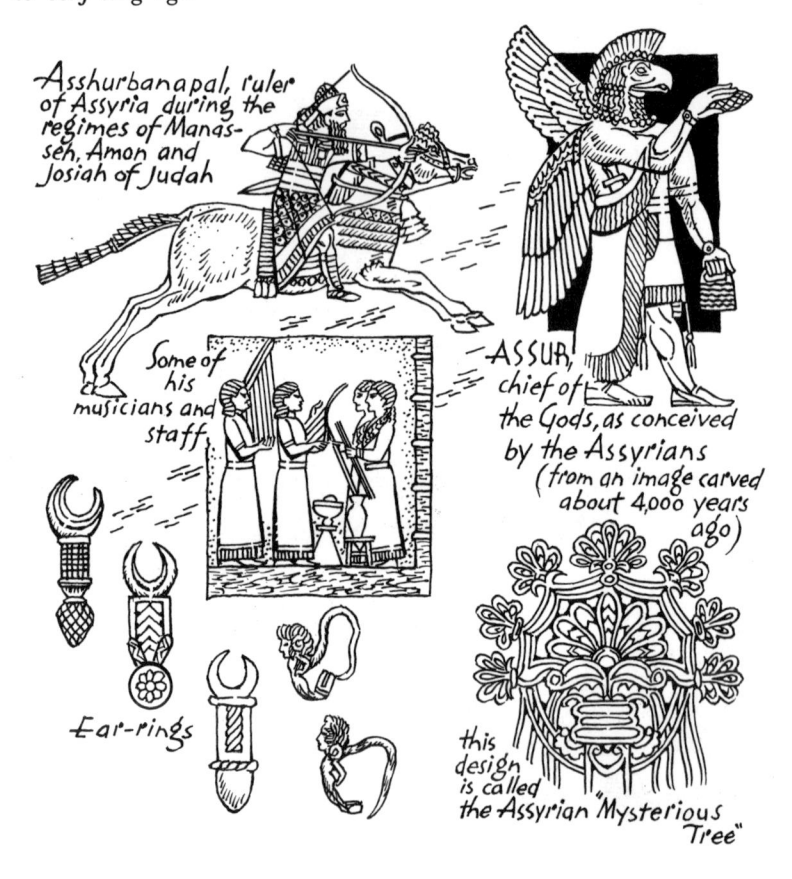

Asshurbanapal, ruler of Assyria during the regimes of Manasseh, Amon and Josiah of Judah

Some of his musicians and staff

Ear-rings

ASSUR, chief of the Gods, as conceived by the Assyrians (from an image carved about 4,000 years ago)

this design is called the Assyrian "Mysterious Tree"

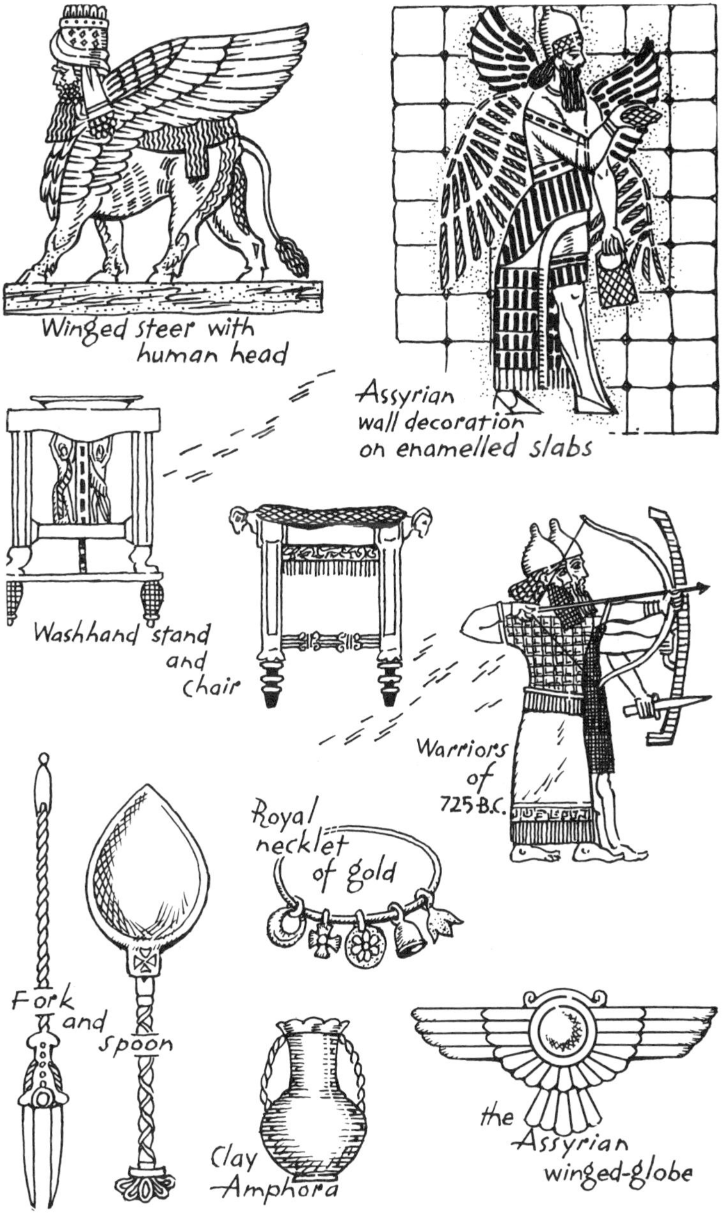
Winged steer with human head
Assyrian wall decoration on enamelled slabs
Washhand stand and chair
Warriors of 725 B.C.
Royal necklet of gold
Fork and spoon
Clay Amphora
the Assyrian winged-globe

III

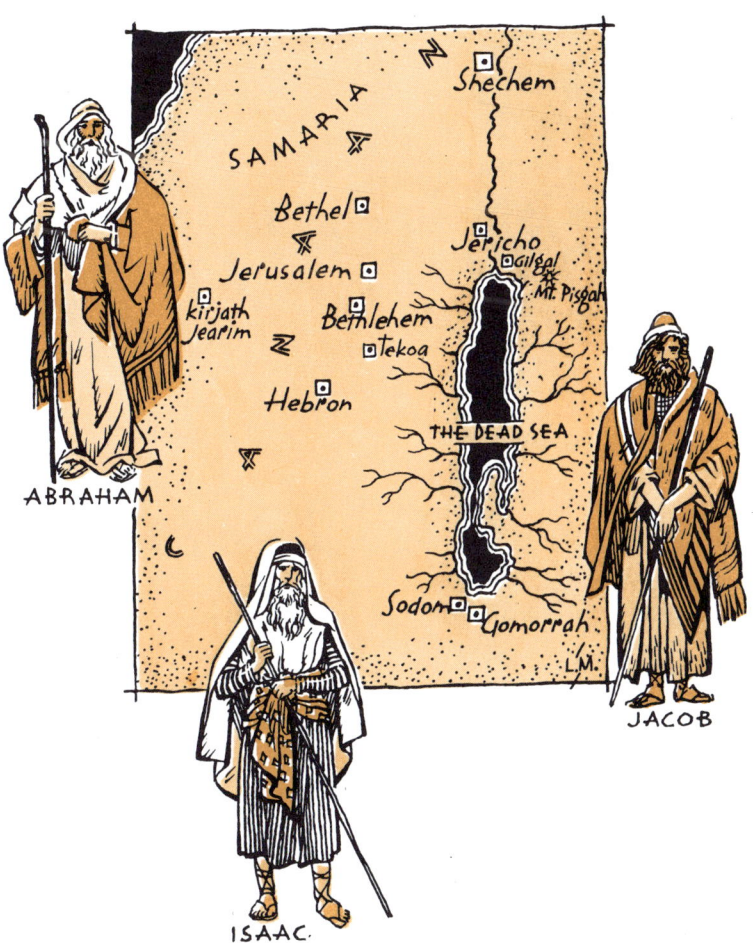

THE PATRIARCHS

CHAPTER SIX

ABRAHAM, FATHER OF THE FAITHFUL

"Leave your home and country, and go to another land that I will show you," said God to Abram. "There I will bless you and make of your descendants a great nation through whom all the families of the earth shall be blessed." And Abram obeyed. Taking with him his father Terah, Sarai his wife, and his nephew Lot and his family, he left the land of Ur and traveled hundreds of miles west until they came to Haran. Here they lived until Terah died. Then they set forth once more until they came down a mountain pass and into a land called Canaan. This was their Promised Land. Turning south, they passed the lake that we know as the Sea of Galilee, and came to Shechem, about at the center of Palestine, where they tried to settle down. But the people were so heathen that they moved some twenty miles farther south to Bethel. The Promised Land did not seem at all promising, and they moved again still farther south. Soon hard times came and Abram and his family group journeyed as far south as Egypt to get food.

Finally they settled down at Hebron; and here God did indeed bless Abram and Lot. In fact their flocks multiplied so fast that there began to be disputes as to pasturage. Abram as family head could have settled these disputes in his own favor; but instead he said to his nephew: "Let there be no strife between us, for we are brethren. Take your choice. If you go to the left, I will go to the right; or if you prefer the right, I will take the left." Lot noticed that the Jordan valley was very fertile and well watered, so he chose that. But in his selfishness he did not notice that his neighbors to the south were terribly wicked and dangerous.

One day while Abram was living peacefully at Hebron, word came to him that there had been a battle between Lot's neighbors at Sodom and Gomorrah, and some rival chieftains to the east who had badly defeated them. Among the captives and booty were Lot and his family and their goods. Though far outnumbered, Abram did not hesitate. Assembling all the men he could muster, three hundred and eighteen, he surprised the enemy by night, defeated them thoroughly, and chased them way past Damascus, rescuing Lot and the defeated kings and restoring their property. As a reward, the kings of Sodom and Gomorrah offered him all the booty; but Abram refused to accept anything for himself. "You shall not say that you have made Abram rich," he replied. He wanted no partnership with these wicked kings, even against their fighting neighbors. But again Lot was not so wise; he moved right back to live among them to his later sorrow.

In connection with this event, we meet up with one of the most interesting and mysterious characters in the whole Old Testament. His name was Melchizedek, and he was a king and a priest, both at the same time. Out of this background of fighting and wickedness, he appeared suddenly and briefly, as a righteous and devout person of importance; and Abram was so impressed that he immediately recognized him as a spiritual brother and high priest of Almighty God. To him Abram presented what seems to be the first recorded instance of tithing in the Bible. Then Melchizedek disappeared again as mysteriously as he came. The New Testament calls attention to this strange and interesting figure, and describes him as a prophetic forerunner of our Lord Jesus Christ, who was "a priest forever, after the order of Melchizedek" (Hebrews 7: 15-17).

Another incident which took place about this time was not so happy. It was connected with God's promise to Abram that he would be the forefather of a great nation. Years had passed, Abram and Sarai still had no children, and it looked as though God's promises would not be realized. Sarai herself first suggested a solution. "Take my servant Hagar for a wife," she told Abram. "If you get a son by her, then the promise will be fulfilled." Abram did so, and there was a child whom they called Ishmael. But from now on there was no happiness in their home; instead there were jealousy and strife, for it has never been according to God's will to have two wives in the same home. When their boy was about ten years old, Hagar took him and ran away. Then God spoke to her out in the wilderness, gave her a special promise of her own, and told her to go back again. But still there was no happiness; it was a divided home.Finally Abram himself had to send her away. She and her little boy almost died way out in the desert; but again God rescued them and gave them a new home and a new start. Ishmael grew up to become the forefather of the Arab people. But ever after, even to this day, there have been tension and ill will between the descendants of Abram and Ishmael, the Jews and the Arabs.

God continued to reassure Abram and renew the promise. To emphasize it, he changed his name from Abram ("exalted father") to Abraham ("the father of a multitude"). He also changed Sarai's name, which means "Yah is Prince," to Sarah, meaning "Princess," that is, in her own right. But as they grew older and older it became more and more discouraging to both of them that there still was no child.   Genesis 12-17

CHAPTER SEVEN

THE TERRIBLE END OF SODOM AND GOMORRAH

One day three men appeared before Abraham as he was sitting at the door of his tent in the heat of the day. Hospitable and generous as he was, he hurried courteously to meet them, and entertained them with the best that his house could provide on such short notice. The visitors turned out to be angels of the Lord; and while they were eating, their spokesman renewed God's promise to Abraham in an interesting way. "Where is Sarah your wife?" he began. "I will surely return to you in the spring, and she shall have a son." Sarah was listening behind the tent door, and she laughed to herself because it seemed too much to believe that at her age she should have a child. The Lord knew she had laughed, and rebuked her. "Is anything too hard for the Lord?" He asked. "At the appointed time, I will return and you shall have a son."

Meanwhile as the guests were departing, Abraham went with them to point out the way. As they stood looking in the direction of Sodom and Gomorrah, the Lord admonished Abraham to remain steadfast in his faith and in the path of righteousness. Then He told him that it was His purpose to destroy those two cities because of their wickedness. Abraham thought of his nephew Lot and his family, and of other decent families that might be there too, and he began to plead for them to the Lord. "Wilt thou indeed destroy the righteous with the wicked?" he asked. "Suppose there are fifty righteous there? Should the righteous fare as the wicked? Far be that from thee! Shall not the Judge of all the earth do right?" And the Lord replied that if fifty righteous people could be found, He would spare the cities. Abraham continued to pray and plead until finally the Lord promised that if even as few as ten righteous people could be found, He would spare the cities for their sakes.

Alas! There was only one family of four, and even that house was divided. Lot and his wife and their two daughters were still on the Lord's side, but the sons-in-law were among the wicked. The Lord's messengers had a terrible time when they visited Sodom that night. But even so it was with some difficulty that Lot and his family were persuaded next morning to leave all their possessions and flee; it seemed so impossible that two such large and prosperous cities would really be destroyed. Then the Lord God rained fire and brimstone upon those wicked cities and destroyed them from the face of the earth. And ever since, they have been an example of what finally happens to people who refuse to obey God's laws of righteousness and decency.

But Lot's wife, even while they were fleeing for their lives, could not get her mind and heart away from the city and the things they were leaving. Looking back, she became a pillar of salt. She too was destroyed with the people she did not want to leave.

the child of laughter

When spring came, Abraham and Sarah were blessed with the birth of a son, just as the Lord had said. Sarah had laughed in unbelief when he was promised, and Abraham had doubtless laughed too, in wonder. But both laughed with joy and gratitude when he came. No wonder that they named him "Isaac," which means "laughter"; he was the child of laughter. And as long as his parents lived he brought laughter and sunshine into their home. Of the three patriarchs, Abraham, Isaac, and Jacob, Isaac's life was the most peaceful. No tremendous events center around his name, but he has always been remembered and loved because of the quiet good that he did. To the end of his days he was a joy and an inspiration to all who had anything to do with him. Isaac is an example of how noise and glamour and excitement are not necessary either to fame or to happiness. To him God also renewed His promise first made to Abraham, that through their family descendants all the world would be blessed; and it is possible in the Bible to follow the line of ancestors, from our Lord Jesus Christ way back to Isaac and Abraham. Thus the promise was kept.

And yet there were tense moments in Isaac's life too. There were, for instance, those unhappy years of jealousy and strife between his mother and Hagar over himself and Ishmael, that have already been told about. But there was an even more unforgettable time up on Mount Moriah, when his father almost slew him as a human sacrifice to the Lord God. The next chapter will unfold that story.

Genesis 18, 19 and 21

CHAPTER EIGHT

ISAAC

The heathens worshipped idols

Abraham lived in the midst of heathens. He detested their idolatry, and especially their practice of making human sacrifices to their horrible gods. He was glad that Jehovah God made no such demands; He was the God of righteousness and love. Then one day the Lord told him to do that very thing! "Take your son, your only son, Isaac whom you love!" He said, "and go to the land that I will show you, and offer him there as a burnt offering." So now it had come to him too! Would he in his devotion to the true God dare to go as far as the heathen did in their obedience to their false gods? If he did, what about God's great promise, which was so intimately connected with his only child? But Abraham did not hesitate. Rising early, and taking with him two servants and young Isaac, he set forth. On the third day they lifted up their eyes and saw the place afar off. "Stay here," he said to the servants, "and I and the lad will go on alone." And they two went on together, Isaac carrying the fire wood, and Abraham the fire and the knife. "My father!" said Isaac. "Here am I, my son," he replied. And Isaac continued: "Behold the fire and the wood. But where is the lamb for a burnt offering?" Abraham's heart was breaking. All he could bring himself to say was: "God will himself provide a lamb for the burnt offering, my son." And they went on together. When they came to the place, Abraham built an altar of stones, and laid the fire wood in order upon it. Then he bound Isaac and laid him upon the altar, and raised the knife. At that moment God's angel called to him: "Abraham! Abraham! Do not lay hands on the lad or do him any harm! For now I know that you truly fear God, and obey Him." And looking up, they saw a ram caught in the thicket; this became their sacrifice instead of Isaac. How we admire Abraham for his faith and obedience! But should we not also praise Isaac for his courage and devotion that day? For, according to the

Bible, he was big enough at this time to have resisted his aging father, and run for his life. Isaac, too, proved himself worthy of the promise. Never again did Jehovah God make this kind of demand of His children; instead He sternly forbade human sacrifice. This incident is a foreshadow or prophetic image of our Lord Jesus Christ, who gave Himself as the last great Sacrifice for the sins of the world.

Some time after this, Sarah died at the ripe old age of a hundred and twenty-seven; and they buried her at Machpelah, where Abraham had bought a family burial plot from the Hittites. Meanwhile, as Isaac grew older, his father became more and more concerned about where the right kind of wife could be found for his son. "Do not marry one of these heathen girls around here," he cautioned his son. So it was decided to send back to their old family home for a suitable wife. For this delicate mission, they chose their oldest and most trustworthy servant, Eliezer. After much prayer and preparation, Eliezer set out, taking with him ten of his master's camels and many choice gifts. When he came to the city of Nahor in Mesopotamia, he stopped at the well outside of the city walls, just about the time the maidens would be coming out to draw water for family use. Then he prayed and waited. He had decided on a certain test to determine the character and worthiness of the girl he hoped to choose. Before long a beautiful and sturdy young woman came out, with her water jar on her shoulder, and drew water and prepared to depart again. "Pray, give me water to drink from your jar," he asked of her, courteously. "Drink, my Lord," she said, lifting her jar down from her shoulder to her hand. "And I will draw water for your camels, too." It was quite a job to draw water for ten thirsty camels. And Eliezer, praying and watching, knew that this was the one! She told him that her name was Rebekah and

that she was the daughter of Bethuel, Abraham's own kin, and that she had a brother whose name was Laban. We shall learn more about him later. Eliezer became their guest that night, and as soon as possible told his errand. He also told about the plan he had used for testing her, and of his prayer. Then he distributed rich gifts, and asked for her hand as he had been instructed to do. Rebekah was very willing to go back with him.

When they finally arrived at a point near home, it was toward evening. Isaac had gone out in the field to meditate; perhaps we can guess whom he might have been thinking about! And Rebekah lifted up her eyes, and when she saw Isaac, she alighted from her camel and said to the servant, "Who is the man yonder, walking in the field to meet us?" Eliezer replied, "It is my master." And she took her veil and covered herself. And Eliezer told Isaac all the things that he had done. Then Isaac brought her into the tent, and she became his wife, and he loved her. So Isaac was comforted after his mother's death. Genesis 22-24

CHAPTER NINE

JACOB AND ESAU

"a plain man, dwelling in tents"

"a man of the field"

Isaac and Rebekah had to wait twenty years for their first child; it was like the experience of Abraham and Sarah all over again. But then God gave them twin boys. The older one they called Esau, meaning "hairy," because he had an unusual amount of hair all over his body, right from birth. He grew up to be a rough fellow who lived out of doors much of the time and was hard to manage. It was evident that he was not suited for the responsibility of passing on the Great Promise, though as the elder son he should have been the one. The younger twin they named Jacob. He was settled and quiet in his ways, and smarter too, and more resourceful. Isaac favored his older boy, and seems to have been blind to his faults. Rebekah favored Jacob, for reasons that are easy to understand. She seems also to have understood better than her husband that it was the Lord's will that the divine Promise should go to the younger son and that he was more worthy of it. The tragedy was that Isaac and Rebekah did not get together and trust God in the matter. So their home became divided and unhappy, and there was rivalry and ill will and scheming that only became worse as time went on.

One day when the boys were growing up, Esau had been out all day and came in tired and famished with hunger. His brother had been preparing some mixed pottage of venison, beans, and lentils. Smelling the delicious odor, Esau exclaimed, "Give me of that red pottage, for I am starving!" "First sell me your birthright," Jacob replied shrewdly. Esau, being very hungry, consented and even sealed the bargain with an oath. He did not take his birthright very seriously, or else he may have figured that this kind of bargain would not "count." But he did not get a chance to forget it. For the story got out and he received the nickname "Edom," which means "red." All this did not help matters any between himself and his brother. At any rate, Jacob and his mother had now gotten Esau's consent to the giving over of his birthright to his younger brother. They had yet to get the father's consent. This was not so easy, because he was on Esau's side. So there was more scheming.

As Isaac became old he became more and more feeble, until finally he was bedridden and blind. One day he decided that the time had come to make a formal declaration of his last will and testament, and of course it would be in favor of Esau. Calling him to his side, he said: "Behold, I am very old; I do not know what may be the day of my death. So, take your bow and quiver and go out and hunt game for me. Then prepare the savory food that I love, and I will bestow the blessing of the first-born upon you before I die." And Esau went. Meanwhile Rebekah had been listening to the conversation, and now became desperate, realizing that what she had feared all along was about to take place. Summoning Jacob, she said: "Go quickly to the flock and fetch me a couple of kids. I will prepare savory food, and you will bring it to your father, just as though you were Esau. Then you will get the blessing, and the birthright will be yours." When Jacob expressed the fear that his father, though blind, might catch on by feeling his smooth skin, and so curse him instead of blessing him, she instructed him to put on Esau's clothing, and arranged parts of the furry skin of the slain animals about his arms and neck. The trick worked, though the old man Isaac was somewhat suspicious. "The voice is Jacob's," he said, "but the hands are the hands of Esau, and the garments are his."

When Esau returned and the deception was discovered, there was a terrible scene; the father too was deeply affected. But the last will and testament could not be recalled; it had to stand. Furthermore, it was recognized, too, as the will of God. Isaac did indeed give Esau an additional and very special blessing. But it was not the birthright blessing, and therefore inferior. So Esau's hatred of his brother grew worse than ever, and he openly threatened to kill him as soon as their father was dead. Esau forgot, or ignored, the fact that both the birthright and the blessing of the promise were by the will of the Lord; and that the birthright had been given over to Jacob by Esau's own consent. It was not long before conditions became unbearable. So it goes in a home when there is not enough love and prayer and obedience to the will of God.

Genesis 25 and 27

CHAPTER TEN

JACOB LEAVES HOME

It was decided to send Jacob back to his mother's people at Padan-aram. Furthermore he was now old enough to be thinking about marriage, and his parents determined that he should not marry a local girl, since they lived among heathen people. Esau had already grieved them by marrying not only one but two such wives.

Discouraged and fearful, Jacob set forth. When darkness came, he lay down on a rock way out in the wilderness and settled down to sleep. That night he had a vision. He dreamed that there was a ladder set up from earth to heaven, and on it angels were ascending and descending. At the top was the Lord who said to him: "I am the God of your fathers. Do not be afraid. I will bring you safely home again, and the land on which you are now resting shall be yours and your descendants'; and they shall be as the sands of the sea for multitude." Then Jacob awoke. "How holy is this place!" he exclaimed. "It is none other than the dwelling place of God." And he took the stone on which he had rested, and set it up as a memorial, and called the place Beth-el, "The House of God." Then he continued his journey, strong and encouraged again.

He had almost reached his journey's end, when he sat down by a well to rest. Among the maidens who watered their sheep at this well, was a beautiful girl named Rachel. She turned out to be the daughter of the very man he was seeking, namely Laban his uncle. Jacob immediately fell in love with her and eagerly accepted the invitation to be a guest at her home. His courtship was crowned with joy and success. But since he had no dowry to offer, he made an agreement to work seven years for her as Laban's hired man. The years went by like so many days because of his love. But alas! When the wedding day finally came, Jacob found himself married to Leah, Rachel's older sister. This deception by Laban was possible because, according to the custom of the time, the groom did not see his bride until the wedding ceremony was over. To win Rachel, he now had to work another seven years. And to that he added six years to earn enough property and flocks to set up for himself. God blessed him richly; but Laban was not above being jealous of this shrewd young man who got the best of him in everything he did, whether it was business or stock raising.

Twenty years had now passed. Jealousy and bickering had made Jacob homesick for his own people and country, and he decided to take his family and possessions and leave. He did so hurriedly and secretly. As soon as Laban discovered his absence, he hastened after him, angry and threatening. But God warned him not to harm Jacob. They met, and parted again, making a covenant with each other, and setting up a pillar in testimony of it. As Jacob drew nearer home his old fear of his brother Esau came over him again, and he decided to try to win him over with presents, which he sent on ahead. Soon word came back that Esau was on the way to meet him with four hundred men. Jacob did not know that they came to make peace, and he was more afraid than ever. Dividing his flocks and followers, he sent men on ahead with more presents, while he remained behind to pray. That night in the darkness, a strange man appeared before him. Perhaps thinking he was being attacked, Jacob challenged him, and they struggled and wrestled until dawn. Gradually it came over Jacob that this was no ordinary match and that there was something supernatural about this stranger. Finally he touched Jacob's thigh and made him lame. Knowing now that he was an angel from God, Jacob clung to him and said: "I will not let you go unless you bless me!" The angel did so, and repeated the promise God had made to him when he left home twenty years before.

The next day, Jacob and Esau faced each other not as enemies but as brothers, and it was a meeting of peace. Both had learned much since those hot-headed days of their boyhood. Later, when their father died, they joined as brothers once more, to lay him away and mourn his passing. But Jacob never felt quite sure that his brother's friendship was strong and lasting; and he decided not to test it by too close or frequent intimacy. The two brothers remained apart.

Meanwhile God blessed Jacob with more wealth and a

large family, including twelve husky sons. Because there were two wives in the home, there continued to be bickering and faction; but God balanced it all with mercy and favor. He changed the patriarch's name from "Jacob," which means "supplanter," to "Israel," which means "ruling with God." All the rest of his life, Jacob limped; it was a painful reminder of that famous wrestling match with the angel, and he never forgot it. But he bore it with all the pride of a soldier; it had proved to be one of the most blessed events in his whole life.

Genesis 28-35

EMBLEMS ON THE STANDARDS OF THE TRIBES

JUDAH — a lion — יהודה	ISSACHAR — a heavily burdened ass — יששכר	ZEBULUN — a harbor — זבלון
REUBEN — a palm tree — ראובן	SIMEON — a sword — שמעון	GAD — an encampment — גד
EPHRAIM — fruit laden bough — אפרים	MANASSEH — a standard — מנשה	BENJAMIN — a wolf — בנימן
DAN — a serpent — דן	ASHER — fruit and grain — אשר	NAPHTALI — antelope running — נפתלי

Num. 2:1–34

Kings' crowns

IV
EGYPT

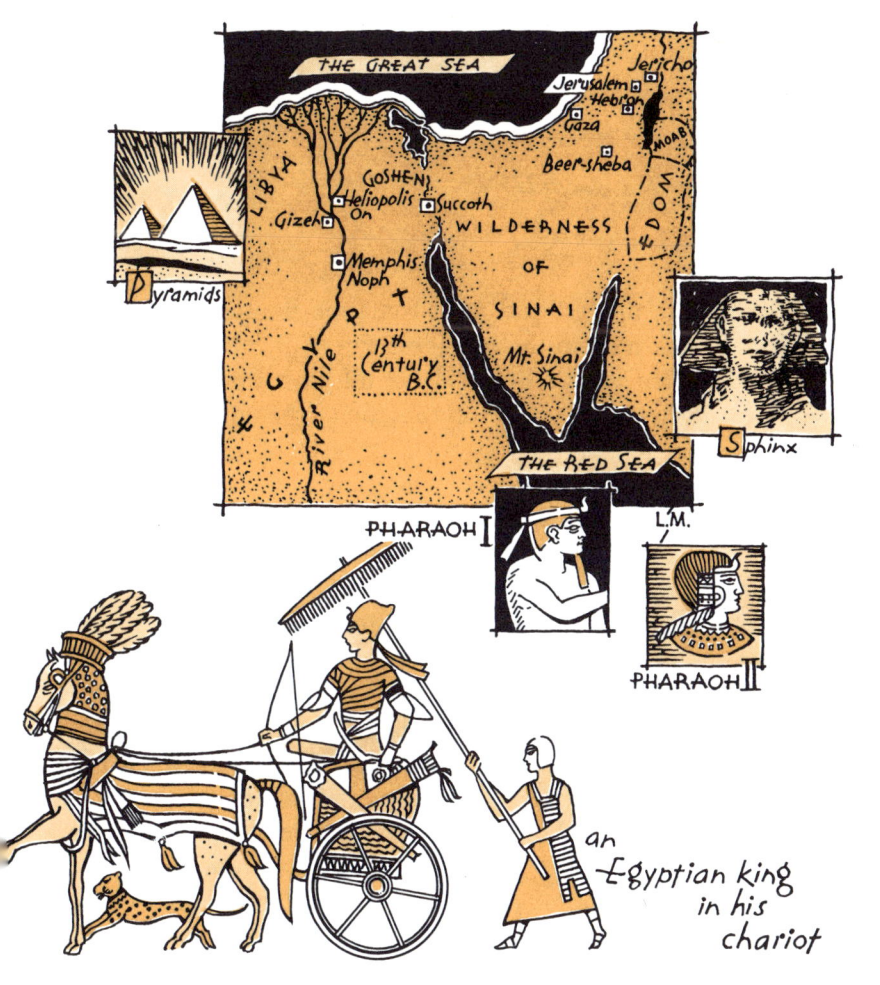

an Egyptian king in his chariot

CHAPTER ELEVEN

JOSEPH

One of the noblest and most romantic figures in all history is Joseph, the next to the youngest son of Jacob the Patriarch. He and his eleven brothers did not all have the same mother, as their father was guilty of the then common sin of polygamy. As a result, there were four sets of children and a household divided by constant wrangling and jealousy. Joseph's mother, Rachel, who was Jacob's favorite wife, died in childbirth when Benjamin was born. Joseph became his father's favorite child, and this was soon noticed by his older brothers, who became jealous of him and hated him. In spite of these tensions and difficult surroundings, Joseph grew up wholesome and unspoiled, strong of body, keen of mind, and devout of soul. He was a dreamer to whom God gave visions of future greatness. These dreams he rather unwisely confided to his brothers, who only hated him the more for them. In one such dream he was tying bundles of grain out in the field, and the sheaves of his brothers gathered around and bowed down to his sheaves. In another dream the sun and moon and eleven stars did the same thing. But the climax of hatred came when his father gave him as a special gift a richly colored and woven garment.

Joseph is sold to the Ishmaelites

One day his brothers were out herding the flocks at some distance from home. Accordingly his father sent Joseph to look them up and report back how they were getting along. Far off they saw him coming, new coat and all! "Here comes the dreamer," they said. "Let us kill him and throw him into one of these pits. Then we will report that a wild beast has devoured him—let us see then what becomes of his dreams!" But Reuben said, "Let us not take his life, but throw him into the pit without shedding his blood." Reuben's idea was to return later and rescue him. His advice was followed. While they were eating, a caravan came by, headed for Egypt. Then said Judah, "What profit have we if we kill our brother and conceal his blood? After all, he is our brother. Let us sell him to these Midianite travellers." They did so, and then smeared his robe with the blood of a goat, and brought it home to their father and said: "See now what we have found, whether it is your son's robe or not." Jacob recognized it and was prostrated with grief and would not be comforted. "I will mourn for him until I am joined with him in the grave!" he said. Meanwhile Joseph was on the way to the land of the Pharaohs, with his captors.

When they entered the fabulous land of Egypt, some thirty-five centuries ago, it already had a couple of thousand years of civilized history behind it. Joseph's eyes saw many of the same pyramids that we can still see there now. Indeed, some of them had already been there a thousand years, sprawled like huge sentinels along the edge of the desert west of the Nile. Everything ran to hugeness and grandeur in this strangest of ancient lands, the bread basket of the world, which owed its own life and existence to the waters of a single river. But there was no share in the grandeur for young Joseph. He was only a helpless Hebrew slave, soon to be offered for sale to the highest bidder at a slave market. Yet he did not despair or become bitter. Instead, he made up his mind to keep his life and heart free from sin, and to remain true to the faith of his fathers. Joseph was bought by Potiphar, a captain in the Pharaoh's own guard.

It did not take Potiphar long to discover that Joseph was no ordinary slave. He learned to trust him completely, and turned over to him all his household affairs. Young and handsome as he was, it did not take Potiphar's wife long to notice him either. She fell in love with him and tried to tempt him into sin with her. But his reply was: "Your husband, my master, trusts me completely and has put everything into my hands. How then can I do this great wickedness and sin against God?" Angry at being scorned, she framed up a charge against him to her husband, who threw Joseph into prison. Never had his fortunes been at so low an ebb. Again, he did not despair, but resolved to trust in God and prove worthy. It did not take long before his virtues won out; the jail keeper made him overseer in charge of all the prisoners. Nevertheless, Joseph remained a prisoner, forgotten by those who could have freed him and by whom his virtues should have been rewarded. But God did not forget him. Meanwhile time passed on.

Genesis 37 and 39

The huge sentinels

Examples of EGYPTIAN ORNAMENT

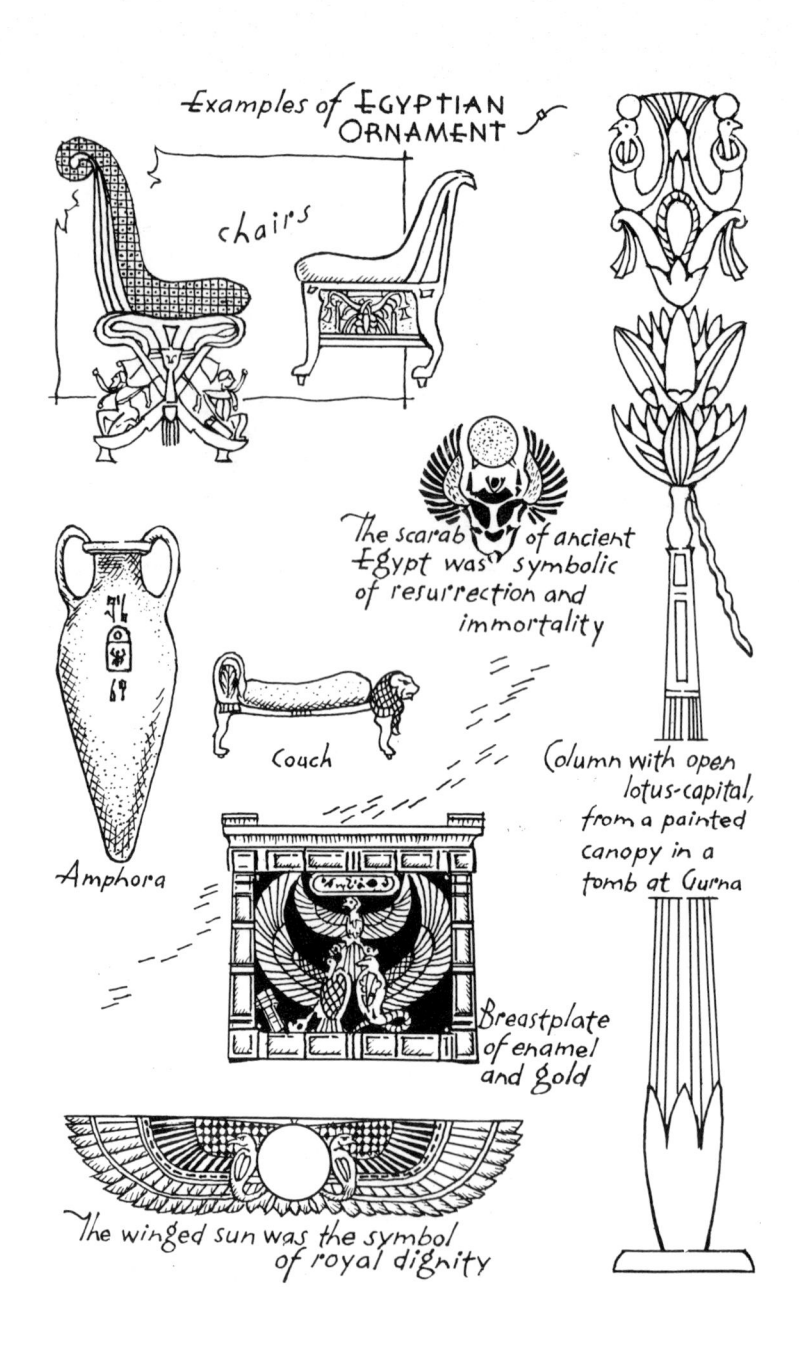

chairs

The scarab of ancient Egypt was symbolic of resurrection and immortality

Amphora

Couch

Column with open lotus-capital, from a painted canopy in a tomb at Gurna

Breastplate of enamel and gold

The winged sun was the symbol of royal dignity

CHAPTER TWELVE

FROM PRISON TO PALACE

the Butler and the Baker

After a while Joseph was joined in prison by two other men of importance, namely the chief butler and the chief baker of Pharaoh himself. One night they both dreamed. In the butler's dream, he was looking at a grape vine, and as he looked it budded into three branches with clusters of grapes on them. He took these and squeezed their juice into Pharaoh's cup and gave to him. Now the chief butler was unable to interpret his dream, so he confided in Joseph concerning it. "This is the interpretation," said Joseph. "Within three days you will be restored to favor and will once more serve Pharaoh as his butler. When this comes to pass and things are well with you again, remember me here in prison, I pray you, and put in a good word for me. For I was stolen out of the house of my father, and am here in prison an innocent man."

The chief baker, noting the ease with which Joseph interpreted the dream, and the happy explanation he gave it, told also his dream. In it he was carrying on his head three baskets of cakes and baked food for Pharaoh. As he did so, birds came and ate up the food in the topmost basket. To this dream, Joseph gave the interpretation that within three days, Pharaoh would have the chief baker taken out of prison and hanged, and the birds would come and peck the flesh from his bones. It happened as Joseph said. The chief baker was taken out of prison and put to death, while the chief butler was released and restored to his former position. But he forgot his promise to Joseph, and did not put in a good word for him with Pharaoh. Two years passed and Joseph was still in prison.

Then Pharaoh himself dreamed. He was standing by the Nile, and out of the river came seven cows, sleek and fat, and grazed along the bank. After them came seven gaunt and scrawny cows, who ate up the fat and healthy ones, but grew no fatter themselves. Then Pharaoh awoke. When he got back to sleep, he dreamed again. This time he saw a stalk with seven ears of grain growing on it, all of them plump and healthy. After them sprouted seven other ears that were thin and blighted. They swallowed up the seven good ears, but remained just as thin and sickly as before.

Pharaoh could not get these dreams out of his mind, and called in all his wise men to try to interpret them. But none of them could help him. Then all of a sudden the chief butler remembered Joseph and how he had interpreted dreams so accurately; and also the forgotten promise to put in a good word for him to Pharaoh. "I remember my faults today," he confessed. Then he told the whole story of his own and the chief baker's dreams. And Pharaoh sent for Joseph in all haste, and had him taken out of prison and brought into his presence. "God will give Pharaoh a favorable answer," said Joseph when the dream was told to him. "God is about to send seven years of great plenty. But after them will come seven years of terrible famine." Then he proposed a plan for storing all surplus grain during the years of plenty, and selling it again during the years of famine, thus not only saving the country from starvation but also making a handsome profit for Pharaoh the ruler. And Pharaoh was so impressed by the interpretation

Joseph interprets Pharaoh's dreams
Gen. 41:25-36

and the plan, and by the personality and character of Joseph himself, that he appointed him food administrator for the whole country, and gave him such power and authority, that he was next only to Pharaoh himself. Thus in one leap, Joseph went from prison to palace, from slave to overseer over the entire nation of Egypt. Truly, God had not forgotten him.

During the seven years of plenty, Joseph was busy building granaries and organizing the country for food conservation, and preparing for the famine that he knew lay ahead. Meanwhile he settled down, married an Egyptian girl, and became more and more identified with the Land of the Pharaohs. But he could not forget his old home and people. To his two sons he gave Hebrew names, Ephraim and Manasseh, and he brought them up carefully in the faith of their fathers. Then came the famine. It extended far beyond the borders of Egypt; and from all corners of civilization people came to buy grain. Even rich and resourceful Jacob and his family began to feel the pinch of hunger. What should they do?   Genesis 40 and 41

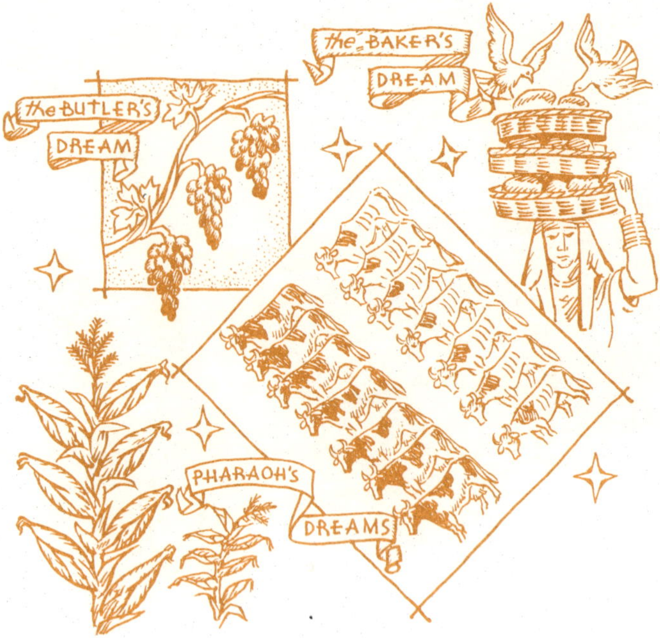
the BUTLER'S DREAM
the BAKER'S DREAM
PHARAOH'S DREAMS

CHAPTER THIRTEEN

REUNION IN EGYPT

The brothers before Joseph

When Jacob learned that there was grain to be had in Egypt, he sent his sons thither to buy. But he did not send Benjamin, the youngest; he could not bear to let him out of his sight. It was before Joseph himself that the brothers appeared when they arrived to make their purchase. He recognized them immediately and was moved, but he did not reveal himself. Instead, he said "You are spies!" and cast them into prison for three days. Then he gave them permission to buy grain and return home, but declared that Simeon would have to remain as a hostage. The brothers were distressed and saw in the order the hand of God for their wickedness toward Joseph. "In truth we are guilty concerning our brother," they said, "and therefore this has come upon us." They did not note that their haughty host understood them and turned aside and wept. They only saw his stern expression when he warned them as they left that they must not come back unless they brought with them their youngest brother Benjamin.

That night when they stopped for rest, each brother found his pay-money placed in the mouth of his sack of provender. Scared and puzzled, they hurried back to Canaan and told their story. Jacob, however, declared that he would never permit Benjamin to leave; he had lost Joseph and he was not going to risk his youngest son on any such dangerous errand. But alas, hunger knows no mercy and the time came when they had to go back. There was no choice but to take Benjamin with them. They also took along double money to make up for what had been returned to them, and brought presents besides.

When they appeared before Joseph, he was again deeply moved, especially to see his younger brother. "Assemble at my house at noon," he commanded. There they were joined by the brother Simeon, and found that a great banquet had been prepared for them. What a feast it was! They were amazed to notice that they had been seated correctly according to age, and that their host also showed other surprising familiarity with them and their family life. He was very generous in the portions they received, but Benjamin received very special portions and attention. It was with happy hearts that they set out once more on their journey back to Canaan.

Soon they again found that the purchase money of each brother had been placed at the mouth of his sack. Filled with foreboding and fear, they were discussing what this might mean, when Egyptian pursuers rode in among them and demanded, "Where is our master's drinking cup?" It was discovered in none other than Benjamin's sack. They were now all placed under arrest and hurried back before Joseph. "Benjamin must remain as my slave," he decreed. Then Judah stepped forward.

the master's drinking cup

Benjamin is brought before Joseph

Protesting that they were innocent of all theft or deception, he told the whole story of Benjamin and their home, and also told about Joseph and confessed their guilt in the way they had treated him. "Let me remain as your slave, and let Benjamin go!" Judah pleaded in conclusion. "If he does not return, it will break his father's heart and bring him with sorrow to his grave."

Then Joseph could stand it no longer. Ordering everyone else to leave the room, he revealed himself to his brothers. With deep emotion, he confided to them: "I am Joseph, your brother! Do not be distressed or angry with yourselves, for God has sent me here before you to preserve life." Then he told them to hasten home and bring Jacob and the entire household back to Egypt. "For there are yet five years of famine to come," he added, and he kissed his brothers and they all wept together for joy and wonder.

The story of Joseph and his brothers spread quickly throughout the court. Pharaoh, too, heard of it and was pleased. "Take your father and your households and come to me," he sent word, "and I will give you the best of the land of Egypt. Take wagons also, but do not bother with your goods; for the best of the land shall be yours." When the brothers arrived home, Jacob would not believe their wild tale. However, when he saw the Egyptian wagons he had to believe. "It is enough," he said. "Joseph my son is alive. I will go and see him before I die." But when they drew near the borders of Canaan, his fears returned; it seemed to him as though he was deserting the Land of the Promise and the Covenant. Only a vision from God could reassure him and get him to complete his journey. "I will go down with you to Egypt," the Lord said. "And I will also bring you up again. And Joseph's hand shall close your eyes when you die."

When they arrived in Egypt, they were well received, and were given the district of Goshen for their possession. Jacob was invited to appear before Pharaoh himself, and was treated kindly. Dignified and unafraid, the old patriarch stood before his ruler, and gave him his blessing. Then he departed to live out his remaining days among his children and children's children, in comfort and honor, and in the faith of their forefathers. But they lived now in a strange land.   Genesis 42-46

Joseph meets his father

V
BIRTH OF A NATION

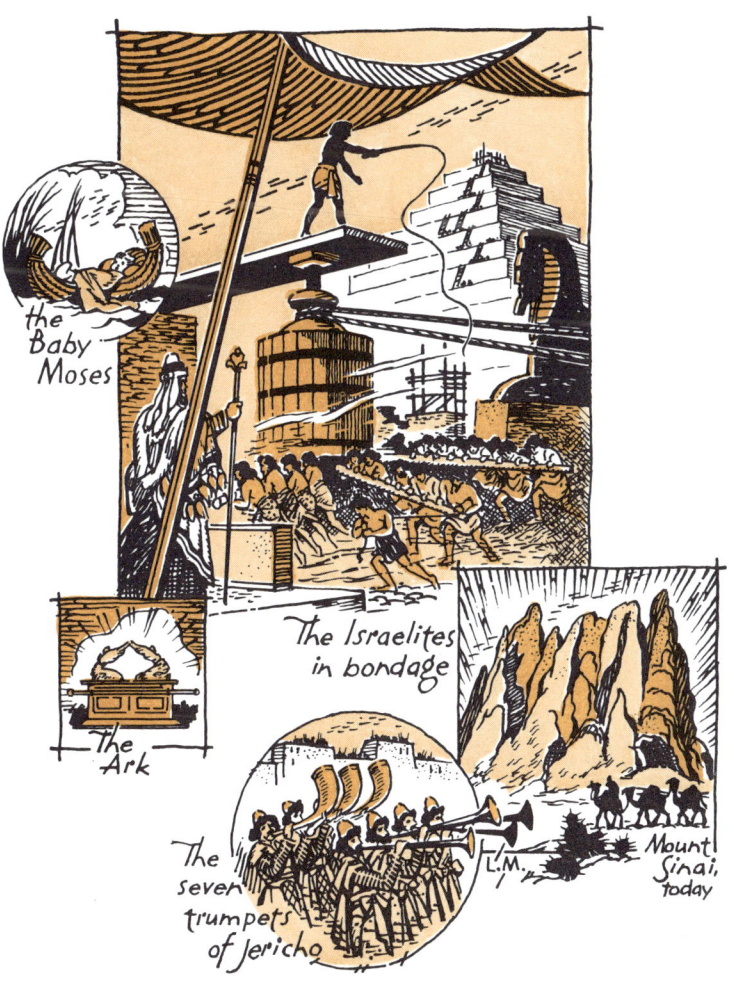

CHAPTER FOURTEEN

BIRTH AND TRAINING OF MOSES

Hebrew slaves

For a while everything went well with the household of Jacob and his descendants. They were thrifty and law abiding and their numbers grew. Then the times changed. A new dynasty which knew and cared nothing about Joseph came to the Egyptian throne. The lot of the Hebrews now became harder and harder, until they were finally made out-and-out slaves. But they were a hardy race, and although brutally treated, they continued to survive and multiply. Finally, in an effort to keep down the Hebrew slave population lest it become too strong, Pharaoh issued a decree that all their male children should be destroyed as fast as they were born. The Israelites had now been in Egypt several centuries, and their lot was hard indeed. It was a wonder that their faith and their remembrance of the Promise were not drowned out completely by time and misery.

Just at this time, there was born in the humble hut of a devout Levite couple, a little boy. He was healthy and beautiful, but to his parents his birth was a calamity on account of the decree concerning Hebrew children. For three months they managed to hide him, but then it became impossible. Finally, in desperation his mother got an idea. She made a little ark or boat, wrapped her baby carefully and laid him in it, and then placed it in the river Nile just at the right time and place where she knew that Pharaoh's daughter would be coming to swim and take her walks. Then she stationed her little daughter Miriam to keep watch. And sure enough! At the customary time Pharaoh's daughter did come down to the river. She saw the little vessel floating among the reeds, and sent a slave to bring it to her. When she saw the beautiful little baby boy, with his coal black hair and large brown eyes, we may be sure that she recognized him easily as a Hebrew child. All the instincts of mother love came over her, and she made up her mind to rescue him and adopt him as her own son. The little girl Miriam was not far away and did not miss a single move. Coming up, she was sent by the princess to find a Hebrew nurse for the child, and we do not have to guess long whom she picked; it was the baby's own mother. Thus, by the grace of God, was born and preserved one who was destined to be among history's grandest figures. He was given the name Moses, which means "drawn from the water."

The baby in the rushes

Moses' early childhood was spent at his mother's knee, and she planted in his soul all that she could of the religious lore and love of his people. This intensive early training played a tremendous role in his later life. His secular education was received at the royal court, and we may be sure that it was generous and complete. But the most practical (and costly) part of his training came to him by harsh experience and hardship. By that time Moses was forty years old.

It saddened and angered him that his people were kept in brutal slavery, and that he could do nothing about it. One day he came upon an Egyptian beating an Israelite. It was doubtless a familiar sight; but he could stand it no longer, and interfered so lustily that he slew the Egyptian. Scared, he hid the body in the sand and told no one. A short while later, he came upon two of his own countrymen fighting. While trying to reconcile them, one of them asked him: "Who made you a prince and a judge over us? Do you mean to kill me as you killed the Egyptian?" Then Moses realized that his deed was known, and he decided to flee. But where could he go? To the west was the desert, to the south the African jungles, to the north the sea. Moses fled east to the hills and pasture country of Midian. This was all the more natural because it lay in the direction of the land of his forefathers, the land of his dreams.

We next find Moses seated by a well in Midian, where the daughters of a certain shepherd-priest came to water their sheep. He helped them do so, and also protected them against the rudeness of some rough shepherds who tried to get their own flocks to the water troughs ahead of theirs. Moses now became the guest of the father of the shepherd girls, whose name was Jethro (also called Reuel in the Bible). Here he settled down and married one of the daughters, Zipporah by name. What a come-down for a prince of the court of Egypt to become a rough wilderness nomad, married to a simple shepherd girl. Another forty years of Moses' life had now passed, and two thirds of his life was gone. But they were not wasted. God was training him in the ways of the wilderness, and this special training was to stand him in good stead later. The quiet and solitude of the desert gave him time for contemplation and prayer and communion with God. Great and difficult tasks lay ahead, and he would have need of spiritual and physical fortitude. Exodus 1 and 2

COMMUNION WITH GOD

CHAPTER FIFTEEN

MOSES' CALL AND THE CONTEST WITH PHARAOH

One day as Moses was tending his flocks, he noticed a bush that was on fire. It burned and burned but was not consumed. Filled with curiosity, he went over to it. Then came a voice: "Do not come near, but remove your shoes, for you are on holy ground." It was the voice of God. He called upon Moses to return to Egypt and lead the Israelites out of slavery and back to the Promised Land of their forefathers. But Moses was scared when he thought of his shortcomings and the hugeness of the task. God reassured him and promised to support him even with miracles, but he still hesitated. Then the Lord bade him cast his shepherd's staff upon the ground. It became a serpent until he took it up again, when it was once more a staff. Then he was told to put his hand into his bosom, and it became white with leprosy. When he put it in again, it was healed. This was God's way of pledging to him divine power and help. But still Moses hesitated, until the Lord had to rebuke him sharply. Then the Lord appointed Aaron, his brother, to be his

THE TEN

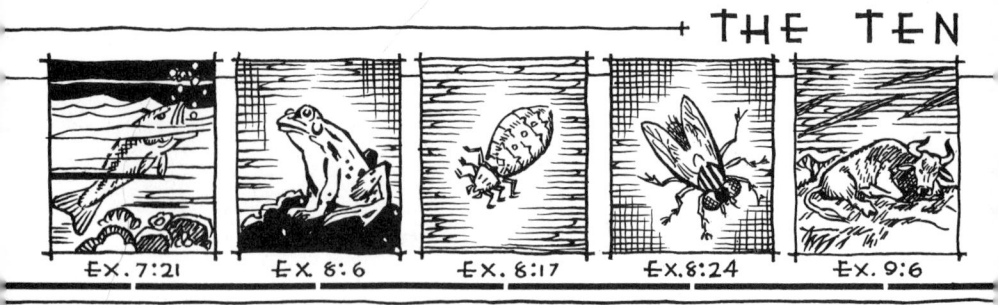

Ex.7:21   Ex.8:6   Ex.8:17   Ex.8:24   Ex.9:6

assistant. Finally, Moses set forth on his great and daring adventure, with Aaron by his side.

Upon arriving in Goshen, they addressed their countrymen at a great religious festival, and Moses was accepted by them as their leader. Now began the great struggle for freedom by a people without arms or weapons, against the power and pride of Egypt. When Moses and his brother appeared before Pharaoh with their petition to leave, the answer was a rough and emphatic No! Instead, Pharaoh ordered heavier burdens than ever to be laid upon the Israelites. Moses turned to God in prayer.

Then began a terrible contest to beat down the stubbornness and cruelty of Pharaoh and obtain permission to depart. Within the space of about one year, God, through Moses, laid upon Egypt a series of ten calamities or plagues so terrific that the Israelites never forgot them. They came in the following order:

1. The turning of the water of the Nile to blood, so that the fish died and the entire country stank.
2. The plague of frogs, coming up out of the river and filling the whole land.
3. The plague of gnats everywhere, as plentiful as dust.
4. Flies that swarmed like clouds into every dwelling, from the humblest hut to Pharaoh's own palace.
5. Pestilence upon all the cattle of Egypt.
6. Boils and sores on man and beast throughout the nation.

PLAGUES

Ex. 9:10   Ex. 9:23   Ex. 10:13   Ex. 10:22   Ex. 12:29

7. Hail that levelled and shattered every growing thing.

8. The plague of grasshoppers that hid the sun with their numbers, and devoured everything in their path.

9. Three terrible days of darkness, when men groped in terror at noonday, and night and day were the same.

Sometimes, as one plague succeeded the other, Pharaoh would seem to relent, only to harden his heart as soon as it was over. At other times he would be truly frightened. But always he reversed himself as soon as the plague had spent itself.

10. The last plague was the most terrible of all. It came after a particularly solemn warning by Moses. To the Israelites, orders were given to be ready to leave in a hurry. "On the fourteenth of this month, at sundown, let each family kill a sacrificial lamb. Then with its blood put a mark on your door posts and lintels. Roast and eat the flesh carefully, without breaking the bones." Thus the Lord instructed His people. The blood was to be a surety that the angel of destruction would pass them by during the terror of that night. The next morning it was found that death had visited the first-born of every family and flock, from cattle shed to Pharaoh's own palace. The Israelites never forgot the tremendous events of that Passover, as they called it. There are references to it throughout the Bible, and it has been for them and their descendants a national festival way down to this day. But it was more than a never-to-be-forgotten historical event. It was a symbol and a prophecy

of the Last Great Passover some day to come, when the Messiah would be the final Passover Lamb, slain on the Cross for the sins of the world, even Jesus Christ our Redeemer.

To Pharaoh and his people, it was a night of horror. Now indeed was his stubbornness beaten down, and his refusals changed into an eagerness to get rid of the Israelites who had brought such calamities upon him and his nation. Thus at last the Hebrews left the land of bondage, with their heads high, with cattle and possessions, and even with gifts in their hands. But the end was not yet.

Exodus 3-12

The Passover on the eve of the Exodus
Ex. 12: 12-14

CHAPTER SIXTEEN

THE RED SEA AND SINAI

It did not take stubborn Pharaoh long to get over his fright at the death of the first-born. "What is this that we have done in letting Israel go from serving us?" he cried. Then, assembling soldiers and chariots, he hastened after them. He overtook them just as they were encamped by a narrow inlet, called the Red Sea. The joy of the Israelites was turned to fear when they saw the Egyptians ready to close in on them. Bitterly they turned on Moses. "Is it because there are no graves in Egypt that you have taken us away to die in the wilderness?" they said. But Moses replied: "Fear not! Stand firm and you shall see the salvation of the Lord." Then he ordered them to prepare to cross immediately. That night under cover of a thick cloud that God placed between them and the Egyptians,

77

and a wind so strong that it blew back the waters like a wall, they hurried across as though on dry land. Next morning the Egyptians discovered their escape and rushed furiously after them. But now the waters were released, and they were drowned, horses, soldiers and all. In the joy of their deliverance, the Israelites held a great celebration at which a song of victory, composed by Moses' sister Miriam, was sung. It is still preserved in our Bibles (Exodus 15).

Moses could now have led his people a short way, straight up the coast to Canaan. But he knew that they were not yet ready, either physically or spiritually, to meet their enemies and to found a great nation. First they had to have experience and an earnest session with God. So he led them south and east toward the rough mountainous country of Horeb and Sinai. It was not long before the unworthiness of the Israelites began to show itself. Instead of being grateful for their freedom and working together to overcome the hardships between them and the Promised Land, they were rebellious and grumbled at almost every step. God was very patient with them. Once when water failed, He directed Moses to strike a certain rock and a spring gushed forth. Another time when the water was bitter, Moses was given power to sweeten it by throwing into it the branches of a certain tree. Farther on, food became scarce. Then God sent a special miracle-bread called manna that tasted like honey, and appeared on the ground at sunrise and disappeared when the sun came up higher. He also sent flocks of quail so that the people might have meat.

Hur and Aaron hold up Moses' hands

Before long they had their first test in battle, when the Amalekites suddenly attacked them without cause. Moses appointed Joshua to lead in battle, while he stood aside on a hilltop to observe and pray. It was soon noticed that as long as his hands were raised in prayer, the fight went well, but when he became tired and lowered them, it went badly for the Israelites. Then Aaron and Hur came to his side and held up his arms until the Amalekites were beaten off and the victory won. Is not this a lesson in the sustaining power of prayer? The Israelites never forgot this battle and its strange manner of victory, though they frequently forgot its spiritual lesson. But Moses had another happy experience too. For when they drew near his old home in Midian, his wife and family and his father-in-law, Jethro, came to visit him.

Finally, about three months after they left Egypt, they reached Horeb and Mt. Sinai. Here Moses ordered them to pitch camp while he went up into the mountain to commune with God and receive further instructions. When they arrived, they were greeted by an earthquake and a storm so violent that they were afraid to come near the mountain. Moses however was not scared and went on up, telling them to wait. He was gone almost a month and a half, for there was much planning to be done. The people became impatient at his long absence, and restless and rebellious. They were not of a mind to be heroic and serve a God whom they could not even see and who gave them such hard things to do. "Up! Make us gods like those the Egyptians have!" they cried to Aaron. "As for this Moses, we do not know what has become of him." Aaron was not the kind of leader that his brother Moses was. Weakly he yielded to their demands; and out of the gold from the earrings and trinkets that they donated, he constructed a golden calf such as the Egyptians worshipped. Then a great festival was held, according to heathen rites and wickedness, and they danced around their golden calf and worshipped it. God and Moses and righteousness and the Holy Land and God's promise to make of them a great nation, were all forgotten. Meanwhile Moses was up on the mountain in communion with God, and planning and dreaming big things for his people. How would it all end? Exodus 14-17 and 32:1-6

"SO MOSES WENT DOWN TO THE PEOPLE" —EX. 19:25

CHAPTER SEVENTEEN

THE GIVING OF THE LAW

When Moses finally returned, he carried with him two tablets of stone on which were engraved the Ten Commandments. They had been given him by the Lord as the foundation laws of His people. As Moses and Joshua drew near the camp, they heard sounds of singing and shouting. Soon they saw the golden calf and the people carousing around it. Hot with anger, Moses threw down the tablets of stone so violently that they broke. Then he strode into the assembly and called Aaron sternly to account. He received the sheepish reply: "You know the people, that they are set on evil. They said, 'Make us gods to go before us.' And I said, 'Let any who have gold, take it off.' And I threw it into the fire, and there came out this calf." In punishment, Moses had the golden calf ground to powder and strewn on the water, and the people were made to drink of it. Then soldiers went through the camp with drawn swords, and before the affair was over, three thousand of the traitors were slain.

Once more Moses went up into the mountain, this time to plead with God for his people. He came back successful, and with two more stone tablets engraved with the Ten Commandments. They are still the basic laws of morality and behavior among civilized people everywhere. Here they are, in the shortened form in which we memorize them:—

Introduction
I am the Lord thy God.

The First Commandment
Thou shalt have no other gods before me.

The Second Commandment
Thou shalt not take the name of the Lord thy God in vain; for the Lord will not hold him guiltless that taketh his name in vain.

The Third Commandment
Remember the Sabbath Day, to keep it holy.

The Fourth Commandment
Honor thy father and thy mother, that thy days may be long upon the land which the Lord thy God giveth thee.

The Fifth Commandment
Thou shalt not kill.

The Sixth Commandment
Thou shalt not commit adultery.

The Seventh Commandment
Thou shalt not steal.

The Eighth Commandment
Thou shalt not bear false witness against thy neighbor.

The Ninth Commandment
Thou shalt not covet thy neighbor's house.

The Tenth Commandment
Thou shalt not covet thy neighbor's wife, nor his manservant, nor his maidservant, nor his cattle, nor anything that is thy neighbor's.

The Conclusion
I the Lord thy God am a jealous God, visiting the iniquity of the fathers upon the children unto the third and fourth generation of them that hate me; and showing mercy unto thousands of them that love me and keep my commandments.

The Israelites stayed in the neighborhood of Mt. Sinai a whole year; and a complete code of laws and observances was worked out for them under the guidance of the Lord. These laws had to do with property, worship, social and ethical conduct, hygiene, food, religious and national festivals, sacrifices, and offerings, and many other things. They are found in the Books of Exodus, Leviticus, Numbers, and Deuteronomy in the Bible. In the New Testament, the Epistle to the Hebrews is very helpful in explaining their symbolism and purpose. The ceremonial laws went out of effect when Christ the Redeemer came. But the Moral Law, centering around the Ten Commandments, is in effect forever. Our Lord explained and reinterpreted it according to His own New Testament standards in the Sermon on the Mount and other passages.

The Sinai wilderness was a harsh proving ground for the Israelites, but it would have been both easier and shorter if they had trusted in God and followed Moses' leadership more faithfully. Instead they continued to be discontented, and complained constantly. Time after time God had to punish them severely for their wickedness and backsliding. Finally at the end of two years, they arrived at Kadesh-Barnea, near the southern border of the Promised Land. They could now have entered and taken it over, but they lacked the courage. When scouts returned from spying out the land, they reported it as indeed excellent but that the people were large and fierce. Immediately the Israelites were panic-stricken and a rebellion was started under the leadership of Korah, to return to Egypt. Not until thousands of people had been slain was it put down. Then God said: "Surely, none of the men who came up out of Egypt, from twenty years old and upward, shall see the Promised Land, except Caleb and Joshua, for they have wholly followed the Lord."

So for the next thirty-eight years, the Israelites became desert nomads, moving about constantly from place to place, in order to find sufficient food for themselves and fodder for their cattle. And yet God blessed them in many ways. Finally when the next generation came of age, it was well trained in the ways of the wilderness, and far more fit to take over the Promised Land and found a new nation dedicated to God. True, they remained grumblers and stiff-necked, but when the period was over, God could remind them of many wonderful blessings, and say: "I have led you forty years in the wilderness; your clothes have not worn out upon you, and your sandals have not worn off your feet."

Exodus 32 and 38
Leviticus, Numbers, Deuteronomy

The Scapegoat
Lev. 16:8-10

CHAPTER EIGHTEEN

THE DEATH OF MOSES

Moses on the top of Mount Pisgah

Once more the Israelites were near their goal. The old generation was now gone, and the new one which had grown up in the desert was hardened by the years in the wilderness and far more fit to do battle and take over the Promised Land than their fathers had been. Only the land of Edom lay between. To its inhabitants, Moses sent messengers requesting permission to pass through their territory. He promised to pay for everything they needed, and not to molest anyone. But the Edomites refused and threatened them. Although the Israelites likely could have forced their way, the Lord reminded them that the Edomites were their kinsmen, being descendants of Esau. So they withdrew and took the long and more dangerous detour up the east side of the Dead Sea instead. Again there was grumbling. Even manna was no longer good enough for them, "and there is no water!" they said. In punishment, God sent up out of the wilderness serpents that bit and poisoned them. But as soon as they repented, He had Moses set up a brazen serpent on a pole, and all who looked to it and prayed to God in faith were healed. Jesus, in the New Testament, said that this serpent was a symbol of Himself on the Cross as the Healer of the Nations.

When the Israelites reached the borders of the Amorites, Moses again sent messengers asking permission to pass through, on the same terms as he had made to the Edomites. Their answer was to rush out to battle, in which the Israelites soundly defeated them and took over their kingdom. Next lay the land of Bashan. Its king was a remarkable giant of a man named Og. They had to fight him too, and they defeated him just as thoroughly and swept on northward. One more obstacle remained, the Moabites. Balak was their king, and he decided to use tricks as well as force to stop the Israelites. He sent for a famous prophet named Balaam to come and lay a curse upon them. Balaam was a heathen and a wicked man, but he was clever and a most unusual person. God would not let him curse the Israelites; instead he prophesied success for them. And in a remarkable oracle, he prophesied of the coming of Christ, calling him "the Star of Jacob" and "the Scepter of Israel" (Numbers 24:17). Before Balaam was killed in battle he gave King Balak some advice that was as shrewd as it was wicked. They could not stop the Israelites with force, he said, nor with lying prophecies. But if they could tempt them into sin, they would call down the wrath of their God and He would destroy them. And so clever were the Moabites in this that they well nigh succeeded. The Bible tells about the scenes of lust and idolatry at Baal-Peor, and God's punishment of them was terrible and never forgotten. The Midianites also had a hand in this disgraceful affair, and Moses destroyed them completely in battle. All the land along the east side of the Dead Sea and the Jordan river was taken over and divided between the tribes of Reuben, Gad, and Manasseh. The first part of the conquest of Canaan was now over.

Moses' life-work was also now over, and his time had come to die. Calm and unafraid he prepared for his end. First he gave a series of addresses to his people, reminding them of God's goodness, reviewing their history thus far, and pledging them to repentance and new zeal. Then he thanked his Lord and blessed his people, tribe by tribe, solemnly and affectionately. One day he went off on his last mountain trip. He set forth all alone up the steep slopes of Mount Pisgah to a place where he could overlook a great part of the Promised Land that he was not permitted to enter or share. He never returned from this trip. Impressively the Book of Deuteronomy closes: "So Moses, the servant of the Lord, died there in the land of Moab, according to the word of the Lord. But no man knows the place of his burial to this day. Moses was a hundred and twenty years old when he died; his eye was not dim nor his natural force abated. And there has not arisen a prophet since in Israel like Moses, whom the Lord knew face to face." Thus died one of the world's greatest men. Born of slave parents, he freed his people from slavery and founded one of the world's most remarkable nations. In the heart of that nation were preserved the divinely revealed prophecies and truths of God. And out of that nation, in the fulness of time, came the greatest Liberator of all, even Jesus Christ, the Saviour of ALL nations and the Victor over sin and death and the power of the Evil One.   Numbers 20-27; Deuteronomy 27-34

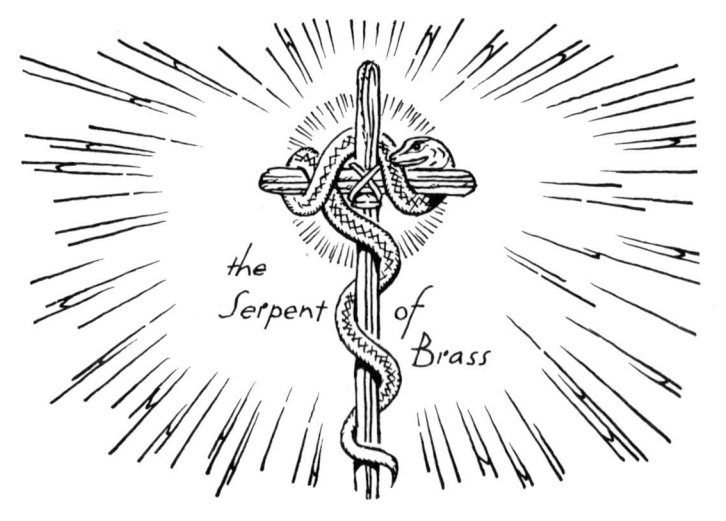

the Serpent of Brass

CHAPTER NINETEEN

THE CONQUEST OF CANAAN

the scouts return from the Valley of Eshcol

The Lord now placed the brave and experienced Joshua in command, and promised to be with him even as He had been with Moses. Joshua immediately prepared to cross the Jordan into Palestine. First he sent scouts on ahead to study the land and the people and to bring back reports. The people and tribes living in the Holy Land at that time are only names to us now—Canaanites, Hittites, Philistines, and others—but they were powerful in their day, and their history went way back in time. Their wickedness and brutality were such that the anger of the Lord was hot against them. Meanwhile the scouts returned. They had indeed had exciting adventures. They had stopped at the house of a woman named Rahab in Jericho, who had befriended them. She was an evil heathen woman, but she had heard of the Israelites and their conquests, and was now learning to respect them and their God. She hid the scouts from their pursuing enemies under some flax straw on the flat roof of her house; and then let them down from the city wall with a rope, her house being built right up against the wall. In return they promised to spare her when the city was taken, and as a pledge the scarlet rope was left hanging from her window.

For their use in worship during the many years of their wandering in the wilderness, the Israelites had erected a sort of open air tent-Church, fenced in by ornate, woven curtains. It was so constructed that it could be easily set up and taken down again. They called this the Tabernacle. It was divided into two rooms, separated by a heavy curtain. The outer one was in constant use for worship, and was called the Holy Place. The other room could be entered only once a year, and by the High Priest alone, on the Day of Atonement, and it was called the Most Holy Place. Here was kept a chest made of precious wood overlaid with gold, and with two golden cherubim facing each other on the lid. It was called the Ark of the Covenant and

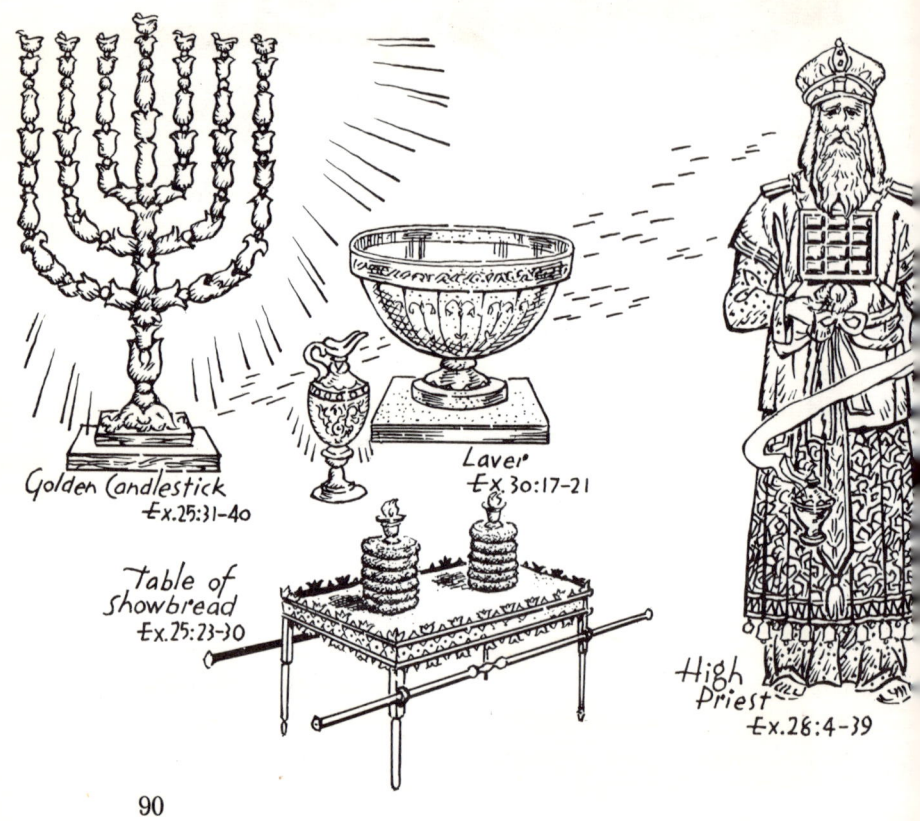

Golden Candlestick
Ex. 25:31-40

Laver
Ex. 30:17-21

Table of Showbread
Ex. 25:23-30

High Priest
Ex. 28:4-39

W
N
S
E
THE TABERNACLE
IN THE
WILDERNESS
Altar of
Incense
Ex.30:1-5
L.M.
Altar of
Burnt Offering
Ex.27:1-8
The ARK
Ex.25:10-22

The crossing of the Jordan

contained the two Tables of the Law and other things of religious value. Joshua now ordered this ark of the Covenant to be carried by priests on their shoulders at the head of the procession, and commanded them to march boldly into the stream of the Jordan. As soon as the priests did so, the waters parted miraculously and the people crossed over as though on dry land.

They set up camp at Gilgal and made it their campaign headquarters. Nearby was Jericho, a strong walled city, which it was necessary to capture before they could go on. And they did it this way: for six days they marched around the city once each day, but did not attack. On the seventh they marched around seven times, carrying the Ark of the Covenant, and blowing trumpets and shouting. At that moment an earthquake rent the walls, and they rushed in. Although the battle of Jericho was won by a miracle, the conquest of Canaan was by no means an easy one. The enemy was defeated by the clever strategy of Joshua, who took advantage of the country's three natural divisions, attacked them one at a time, and conquered them. But the land was not completely subdued until several centuries later under Saul, David, and Solomon. The Israelites did not fully succeed because they failed to obey orders properly, and because of their sin. One of their costliest mistakes was to permit enemy groups and cities here and there to continue living right in the midst of them. These became a snare and a thorn in the flesh to Israel for many generations to come.

Next, Joshua turned to the great task of dividing up the land among the various tribes. There were to be twelve states or divisions, named after the ten sons of Jacob and the two sons of Joseph. The Levites were to dwell in special cities and be supported by the other tribes, since they were to be in perpetual charge of tabernacle and temple worship. By this time Joshua was old and his time had come to die. He prepared for his end with the same calmness and devotion that Moses had shown before him. In two stirring addresses he bade farewell to his people, reminding them of God's continued goodness toward them and of His ancient promise to Israel. The people re-dedicated themselves and promised to be faithful. Shortly thereafter the brave old hero died and was buried at Ephraim, near the grave of Eleazar his high priest who had succeeded Aaron. And the embalmed bones of Joseph, which the Israelites had carried reverently with them ever since they left Egypt, also now finally found their last resting place, according to his dying wish, in the ancient family burying plot which had been bought and laid out by their forefather Jacob, long centuries before. Thus, bound to each other by the pledges of the living and the bones of the dead, the Israelites prepared to face the future in their new Land of Promise. What would it be like, with the old heroes gone? The Book of Joshua

VI
A STRUGGLING KINGDOM

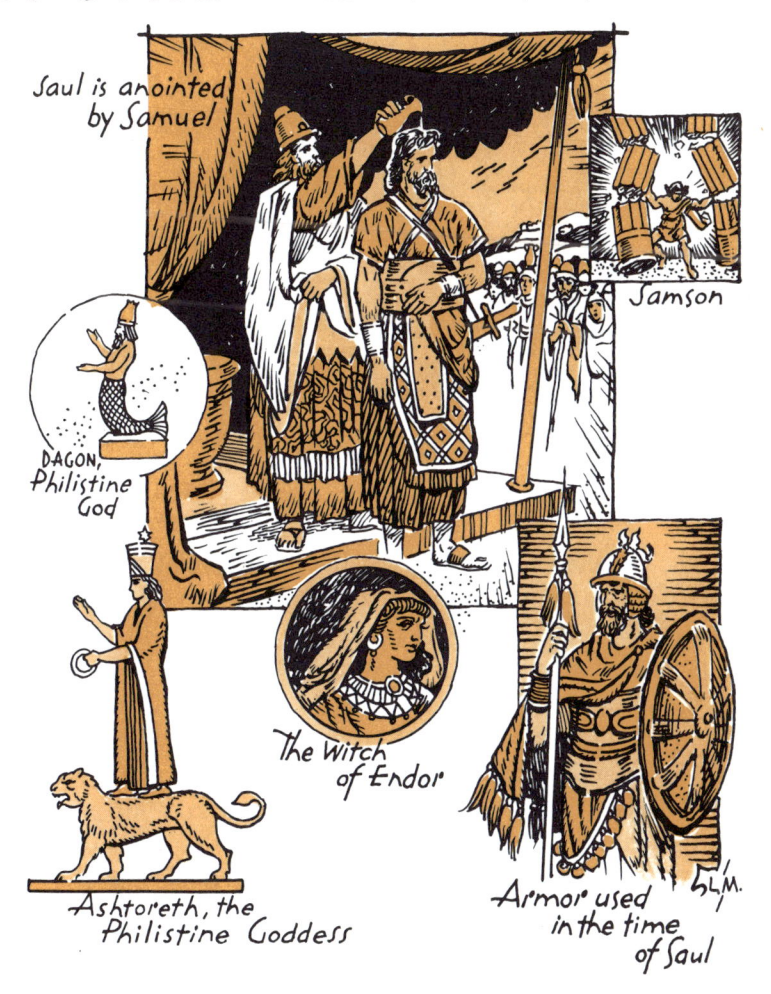

CHAPTER TWENTY

THE JUDGES

Gideon chooses the three hundred
Judg. 7:5-7

As long as there were any of the old wilderness veterans left, the Israelites continued on the whole to obey the Lord. But when they died, the people fell away more and more. As a result, the heathen tribes around them conquered them time after time and made their lives miserable. Then they would cry to God, and He would forgive them and send brave leaders to save them and give them a new start. The Bible calls these heroes Judges.

One of the greatest was Gideon. He was a farmer. One fall, after the Midianites had been plaguing the country for seven years, the Lord called on him to go forth and save his people. He started by destroying the heathen idols right in his own community. Then he called for a general uprising, and thirty-two thousand men came forward. But to show his faith in the Lord, and get rid of the unfit, he invited all who were afraid to return home. Two thirds of them did so. But even eleven thousand were too many, and he finally cut them down to three hundred. He gave each one of these soldiers a trumpet and a jar with a lighted lamp in it. Then in a surprise night attack, they stole up on the Midianites, crashed their jars to pieces, blew their trumpets, and with a shout charged in on the enemy. The Midianites were panic-stricken and fled in confusion. The Israelites never forgot this exploit. Several centuries later, the prophet Isaiah referred to it, and in the New Testament the Epistle to the Hebrews also speaks of it and its hero, Gideon. Gideon would not let them make him king, but he was judge over Israel for forty years.

As time went on, even the champions of the Lord became influenced by their surroundings and the age in which they lived, and on occasion could be crude and rough in their ways. The wonderful thing is that the Lord could still make use of them. An example of this kind was Jephthah. He was the son of a harlot and grew up the hard way, even being banished by his people. But he could not forget their sufferings. In his day it was the Amorites that were grinding Israel. Having been made chief by his countrymen, he went forth to battle. In order to make victory more sure, he made a foolish and reckless vow that if they won he would sacrifice the first person that came to meet them on their return. It turned out to be his own beloved daughter. Bravely she assured him that she was not afraid to die for her country in this way, and urged him to keep his vow. This of course did not make it right. But hers was another brave deed that the Israelites never forgot.

Women could also become Judges. Deborah was one of them. She was also a prophetess. And in that age of fear and danger, she had to accompany the army herself before its captain, Barak, dared to go out against the enemy. They came back victorious.

Israel's most persistent enemy was the Philistines. They were always attacking, and for considerable periods of time, ruled over the Israelites. At this time there grew up a remarkable and strong young man by the name of Samson. He was a Nazarite, that is, he had dedicated his life in a special way to

Samson and the Gates of Gaza

God. He lived a healthy outdoor life, abstained from strong drink and other vices and as a token allowed his hair to grow long and uncut. He grew into a fearless giant of a man and a loyal patriot. But he was also reckless and impulsive, and would often forget his Nazarite vow. He was constantly taunting the Philistines, of whom he was not one bit afraid. One time he slew, with only his two bare hands, a young lion that came at him. Another time he caught several hundred foxes and used them as firebrands to set fire to the Philistines' grain fields. Another time he went boldly alone into the midst of the Philistines at Gaza, and spent the night there. When he left in the morning, he pulled up the huge gates of the city right out of their sockets, and lugged them up the hill and left them there. But the wiles of a woman finally got him. Delilah, a Philistine woman, enticed him, and while he slept she cut off his hair, the emblem of his strength, and turned him over to his enemies. They put out his eyes and set him to turning the huge millstone that ground their grain for flour. Occasionally they would haul him out at festivals and exhibit him and make fun of him and his God. Meanwhile his hair grew out again and his strength came back. One day they again took him into their theater to goad and taunt him. The house was packed with people. Getting the young lad who led him in to show him where he could stand between the two main central pillars that held up the roof, he prayed to God and pressed against them with all his giant might. The pillars collapsed, and the whole roof fell in. "The dead that he slew at his death were more than they that he slew in his life," says the Book of Judges. So lived and died another champion in those wild rough years of the Judges. They lasted about three centuries. Sadly the Book of Judges closes: "In those days, there was no king in Israel; every man did what was right in his own eyes."

The Book of Judges

CHAPTER TWENTY-ONE

RUTH

But conditions during this time were not entirely bad. There were periods of peace too; and there were many who loved the Lord and lived good lives. A beautiful example of this is told in the book of Ruth. Ruth was a kind and faithful girl, whose love story is as wholesome as it is interesting. She lived toward the close of the long period of the Judges.

The story begins with her mother-in-law Naomi. There were hard times and famine in Bethlehem-Judah, where she and her husband and their two sons lived. In fact the times became so desperate that the only solution they could find was to move away into the land of Moab. There, after ten hard years, the husband died. The sons died also, leaving their widows and the mother-in-law, Naomi, poorer than ever. Naomi's heart now began to yearn for her old home again, among her kinsmen and the chosen people. She decided to move back, and her two daughters-in-law, Orpah and Ruth, started out with her. But it did not seem right to her that they should have to leave their own land and go back with her to what was a foreign country to them. She said therefore: "Go, return, each of you, to your own mother's house. May the Lord deal kindly with you, as you have dealt with the dead and with me." Then she kissed them, and they all lifted up their voices and wept. Orpah was finally persuaded to turn back. But Ruth refused. "Entreat me not to leave you," she said, "for where you go I will go, and where you lodge I will lodge; your people shall be my people and your God my God. Where you die, I will die, and there will I be buried." So they came on together.

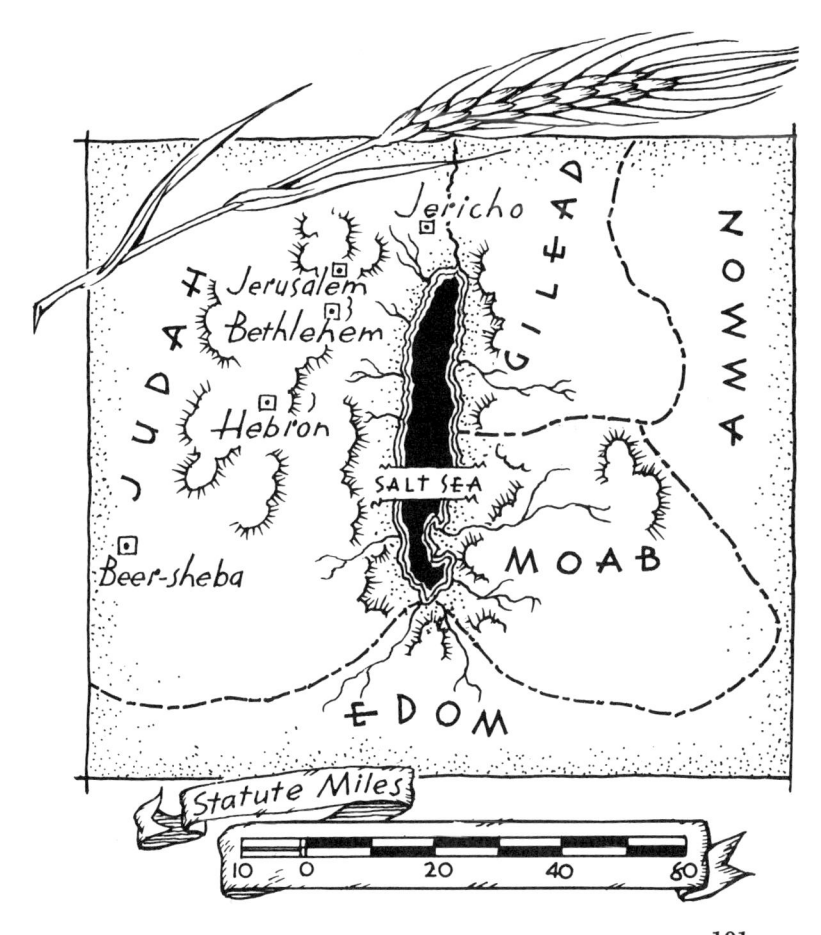

It was at the beginning of barley harvest when they arrived at Bethlehem-Judah. Many of Naomi's old friends and neighbors were still there. They recognized her and noticed that sorrow and time had left their marks upon her. Gathering about her, they said: "Is this the Naomi that we used to know, whose name was "Pleasant"? Sadly she replied: "Call me not 'Naomi' [Naomi means Pleasant]. Call me 'Mara' [Bitter], for the Lord has afflicted me. I went away full, and He has brought me back empty." Prospects did not look very encouraging when she arrived in her homeland again.

Israel had a splendid law that when the grain was harvested in the fall, the corners of the fields were to be left untouched so that poor folks could come and help themselves to what was left, without paying. Now, to eke out a living and at least have some food, Naomi was obliged to send Ruth out to follow the reapers in this way, and to glean what she could of what they left. It chanced that the first field she came to was that of a wealthy squire named Boaz, who was a relative of Naomi through her dead husband. He soon noticed this beautiful and well-behaved young woman and asked about her. Upon learning her story, he called her and said: "Do not go to another field, but remain here; and stay close to my maidens. I have charged the young men not to molest you. And when you are thirsty, go to the water vessel and drink." Humble and surprised, she replied, "How is it that I have found favor in your eyes, and why should you take notice of me, a stranger and a foreigner?" Then Boaz told her that he had learned all about her and her faithfulness to her mother-in-law, and her kindness and virtue. "The Lord repay you for what you have done," he said, "under whose wings you have come to take refuge." Then he instructed his men, not only to let her glean freely and unharmed, but to pull out grain from their bundles, and leave for her to pick up, so that she would be sure to get plenty. That night, when Ruth returned to Naomi, she had all the grain she could carry.

It did not take Naomi long to observe that Boaz was falling in love with Ruth, and she with him. Naomi was very happy about it, and with a mother's intuition furthered the courtship with discretion and wisdom. Boaz treated Ruth with respect and kindness, and by the end of the harvest they were married.

God gave them a son, whom they named Obed, which means "serving." Perhaps it was in memory of those humble days when Ruth was a poor young woman in a foreign land and he was the rich countryman who fell in love with her. It is interesting to note that Obed was the father of Jesse, and Jesse was the father of the great king David. And David, in turn was one of the forefathers of the Lord Jesus Christ. Thus it was God's gracious will that Ruth, who was not even an Israelite, but a Moabitess, was privileged to become one of the ancestors of our Redeemer, according to His earthly genealogy.

Slowly and wearily the period of the Judges dragged itself to a close, and the first glimmer of changed and better times began to appear. The Book of Ruth

CHAPTER TWENTY-TWO

THE LAST OF THE JUDGES

Hannah and Samuel before Eli the Priest

Eli was now judge and high priest. Personally he was a righteous and devout man but he had no control over his two sons who were his assistants. They were dishonest and dissolute, and a disgrace to church and state. Never had spiritual decency been at so low an ebb in Israel. Meanwhile Eli was very old and the time came when his successor would have to be chosen. Who should it be? It was evident that it could not be any of his sons.

One day there came to worship at the Tabernacle a young woman named Hannah, wife of a God-fearing Israelite whose name was Elkanah. As she prayed, she wept because they had no children; and she vowed to the Lord that if He would grant them a son, she would dedicate him to the service of the Tabernacle. Her prayer was answered, and they called their child Samuel, which means "named of God." When he was six years old, true to her promise she brought him to the Taber-

Taking the Ark of the Covenant into battle

nacle and turned him over to Eli to be brought up. Little Samuel slept right in the building itself.

One night the Lord called to him repeatedly and finally told him that because of the wicked conduct of the House of Eli, the sons would be severely punished. God was calling Samuel to be judge and priest in Eli's place. Sadly but obediently, Eli acknowledged the guilt of his sons and bowed to the will of the Lord. Some time later there was again war with the Philistines. To help them win, as they thought, the Israelites were permitted to remove the sacred Ark from the Tabernacle and carry it with them into battle. The result of this blasphemy was the opposite of what they expected. They lost the battle and many people were slain, including Eli's own sons; and the sacred Ark was captured by the enemy. When the news of the battle and the taking of the Ark was reported to Eli, he fell backwards out of his seat, breaking his neck, and died. The Ark, after many adventures, was finally returned by the Philistines.

Samuel now succeeded Eli as judge and high priest. He accomplished many things for his people. He started reforms and raised the standards of morality and decency. Schools for prophets were begun in his day, and he made regular trips throughout the land as judge and overseer. But there were two things he was unable to do. He was unable to give Israel peace and security from her enemies; and he could not control and discipline his own sons, even as Eli had been unable to.

In time people noticed this and it became evident that some change would have to be made. "Look!" they said to Samuel, "you are getting old, and your sons do not walk in your ways. Give us a king, therefore, like all the other nations have!" Samuel tried to dissuade them from the dangers of having a dictator, but they would not listen. So, after praying, and receiving a command from the Lord, he set about finding a proper king for his people. At this time there was living in the district of Benjamin an influential and godfearing farmer by the name of Kish. Among his stalwart sons, he had an especially apt and goodly one named Saul. One day some of the farm animals went astray, and he sent Saul and a servant out to look for them. For two whole days they wandered up and down the countryside without finding them. The third day they came to the community where Samuel lived. They decided to visit the prophet and ask him to help them locate the animals. Saul did not know that God's hand was in this whole incident, and that He had a special purpose in it. Meanwhile Samuel had been instructed by the Lord to make Saul his choice and to anoint him as king. When he arrived, Samuel entertained him royally, and ended the visit by declaring him king-to-be, to Saul's own great astonishment. "Am I not a Benjaminite, from the least of the tribes of Israel?" he protested. "And is not my family the humblest of all the families of Benjamin?"

His final official choice and anointing were just as interesting. Samuel called all the people together. Then by the ancient custom of casting lots through a process of elimination, they left the guidance of the lots to God. The choice fell upon Saul. But when they looked around for him, he was nowhere to be found; overcome by stage fright, he had hidden himself among the baggage. When they found him and stood him up before his people, however, he was every inch a king. In build, bearing, and bravery he was head and shoulders above every one of them. "Long live the king!" the people shouted. But some of them brought him no present and gave him no homage. Saul noticed this but said nothing. It would have been well if he had continued in the humility and attitude with which he began his kingship.

I Samuel 1-10

Site of Shiloh where the Tabernacle was, in the time of Samuel

CHAPTER TWENTY-THREE

KING SAUL

Before Saul had even entered upon his reign, a crisis came up to test his courage and leadership. The Ammonites, from east of the Jordan, suddenly attacked Jabesh-Gilead, and added insult to injury by taunting the Israelites about their helplessness and daring them to find a leader who could do anything about it. Saul was busy plowing when the news came. Stopping his oxen right then and there, he slaughtered them in the furrow where they were standing, and sent a piece of the carcass to each of the tribes of Israel, with the ominous words: "Whosoever does not come out after Saul and Samuel, so shall it be done to his oxen." With amazing speed an army was gotten together, and Saul fell upon the enemy with such fury that they were completely routed.

Saul next turned on the Philistines; but the Israelites had been so bullied and beaten by them that at first the support he received was slow. Then Jonathan, Saul's own son, led off with an attack so brilliant and successful that the whole nation was thrilled. But now we already begin to notice two traits in Saul's character that were destined to prove his undoing. The first was his jealousy and hot temper. It cropped out in this campaign. Instead of applauding and rewarding Jonathan's exploit, he threatened him with death for a breach of discipline so slight that it was unworthy of notice. And he would have carried it out too, if the army had not rebelled on Jonathan's behalf. The second trait was in the form of a disease that has gripped many a leader since Saul's day. It was lust for power! It showed itself in a determination to dictate to both church and state. Samuel sharply reprimanded him, but the only result was a growing rift between the two, and between Saul and his God. Saul's next campaign was against the Amalekites. It, too, began very successfully. He defeated them but stopped their pursuit in order to gather plunder, and so let the enemy escape. God warned him sternly against warfare for plunder,

Warfare for plunder

instead of self-defence, but it did no good. From now on, Saul acted more and more on his own, without regard to either God or his own best advisers. So the Lord marked him for rejection and bade Samuel seek out another and more worthy king.

Again there was war with the Philistines. This time they had a champion. And what a champion! He was a giant in size and strength and brutality, and came from a family of giants. As the armies faced each other, he strutted forward between the battle lines and dared the Israelites to send a man to fight him.

111

Saul was at his wit's end and offered a fortune and his own daughter besides, to the one who could dispose of the monster. Just then there stepped into the scene a ruddy-faced young lad who offered to take on Goliath, the Philistine giant. His name was David. He had been sent with supplies from home to his older brothers who were in the army. "Who is this uncircumcised Philistine, that he should defy the armies of the living God?" he exclaimed as he watched Goliath strut and boast. "I will go and fight him!" His brothers ridiculed him, and Saul could hardly believe his eyes and ears when the lad stepped forward. He refused the king's offer of armor and weapons; he would have to fight him his own way, he said, with the weapons he was most used to. Then he took his shepherd's staff and his sling, chose five smooth pebbles from the brook, and stepped into the arena. These, and his faith in God, were all the weapons he needed. When Goliath saw the lad coming toward him, his disdain knew no bounds. "Am I a dog, that you come at me with sticks?" he shouted. "Come to me and I will give your flesh to the birds of the air and to the beasts of the field!" And David replied: "You come against me with sword and spear; but I come to you in the name of the Lord of Hosts whom you have defied; and this day will He deliver you into my hand." Then he fitted a stone to his sling, and let drive. The stone sank into the giant's forehead and he fell on his face. Then David ran to him, pulled Goliath's own sword from its sheath, and dispatched him with it. The enemy fled and the Israelites pursued them.

"Who is this youth?" Saul asked his captain, Abner, in amazement, after the fray was over. And Abner replied, "As your soul lives, O King, I cannot tell!" Only after summoning the lad himself, were they able to find out who he was. "I am David, the son of your servant Jesse the Bethlehemite," he replied. And Saul fell in love with him, and would not let him return home, but appointed him to be his armor bearer. David was soon to learn however, what it meant to be a praised and popular hero under a jealous and neurotic king. A song was made up and sung from one end of the country to the other. It went like this: "Saul has slain his thousands, but David his ten thousands." When Saul heard it, he was angry and sick with jealousy. "They have ascribed to David ten thousands, while to me they have ascribed only thousands," he said. "What more can he have but the kingdom?" And from that time on Saul eyed David ominously. I Samuel 11-15, 17

Warrior of David's time

CHAPTER TWENTY-FOUR

DEATH OF SAUL

Young David's position in Saul's household was indeed a dangerous one. First he himself knew that he was to take Saul's place some day, and Saul suspected it. David could not forget the time when Samuel had visited his father's farm and had chosen the shepherd lad over the heads of all his brothers, anointing him king-to-be over Israel. In the second place, there were times when King Saul became mentally deranged and acted like a maniac, and it was dangerous to be near him. And yet, in his better moods, his conscience would bother him and he would feel sorry. David's childlike faith in God, his purity of life, his good looks and winning personality, and not least his music, impressed his master even though they were a rebuke and a reminder to him of his own failings. Many a time David wooed Saul out of his moods with his harp and his song. But finally even these failed. Twice the king hurled his spear at him while he sat playing, and it became impossible to go on. Through it all David behaved with a respect and forbearance that were marvelous. There was one person at least in the family that accepted him without reservation. That was Saul's son, Jonathan. The love of these two for each other forms one of the famous friendships of history.

One day after a terrific scene at the dinner table, David had to flee for his life, and from then on he was an outlaw. Hiding in caves and in the wilderness west of the Dead Sea, a ragged company of other outlaws gathered around him that he gradually welded into a well disciplined regiment. He used it in self-defense, in guerilla warfare against his country's enemies, and in preparation for the day when he would be called upon to become king; but never against Saul, whom he continued to treat with respect and chivalry. Many were the stories preserved in after years concerning this period. One time when the king with three thousand men was trying to track down David with his ragged four hundred, David and a trusty servant stole right into their midst during the night. Saul's spear was sticking upright in the ground beside him as he slept. "Let me smite him with his own spear," whispered Abishai, David's companion. "I promise you that I shall not need to smite him more than once!" But David replied sternly: "Destroy him not! For who can put forth his hand against the Lord's Anointed and be guiltless? He will die when his time comes."

Slowly the span of Saul's kingship wore itself to a close. It was a long one, at that, forty years. The end came in a climax of tragedy. There was

David spares Saul's life

Mount Gilboa, from Shunem

war with the Philistines again. They were encamped at the foot of Mount Gilboa, and above them and a few miles off were the Israelites. Saul had an uneasy feeling that this would be his last battle. He had called on God but received no answer. And no wonder, for Saul, in another one of his frenzies had just prior to this massacred eighty-five of Jehovah's priests. In the old days he could go to Samuel. Samuel was hard and brutally frank, but he was honest and constructive. Alas! The old prophet was dead long before this. But perhaps he could talk to Samuel anyway, through a medium or witch! Saul's diseased mind seized on the idea, and he acted.

Late on the night before the Battle of Gilboa, King Saul and two servants knocked at the hut of Israel's last lone witch who still plied her trade at Endor. A few hours later they stumbled away again. The witch-hag had indeed given an answer, and a voice from the dead had spoken: "Why have you disturbed me? For the Lord has become your enemy. He has torn the kingdom out of your hand and given it to David. And tomorrow you and your sons shall be with me." At the words king Saul had fallen headlong, senseless upon the earth. Thus the battle of Gilboa was lost before it was begun. The next night saw valley and mountain littered with Israelite dead, with Saul and his three sons among them, and brave, noble Jonathan in the midst. During the last moments of the battle Saul had thrown himself on his own sword rather than be taken alive by his enemies; and his armor bearer had followed him. When the Philistines found the bodies of Saul and his sons, they stripped off their armor for trophies. Then they cut off Saul's head and carried the bloody torso and those of his two sons to Beth-shan and fastened them to the city wall in horrible triumph. When the citizens of Jabesh-Gilead heard the grisly story, they remembered the time, forty years before, when Saul had left his plow to come and rescue them in the fair morning of his early kingship. And their men arose, travelled all night, and cut down the bodies and carried them back with them. Then they burned them and buried the bones under a tamarisk tree in Jabesh-Gilead, and fasted and mourned seven days.

Thus ended the tragic reign of Israel's first king. And yet he did much for his country. He found Israel a scared and broken people; he left it well on the way toward becoming a united nation, in spite of the defeat that ended his life. He could have done much more, for he had the courage, the strength, and the talent. But he could not govern himself, and he would not let the Lord guide his life. Alas! for men like Saul!

I Samuel 18-31

a Tamarisk Tree

VII
ISRAEL'S GOLDEN AGE

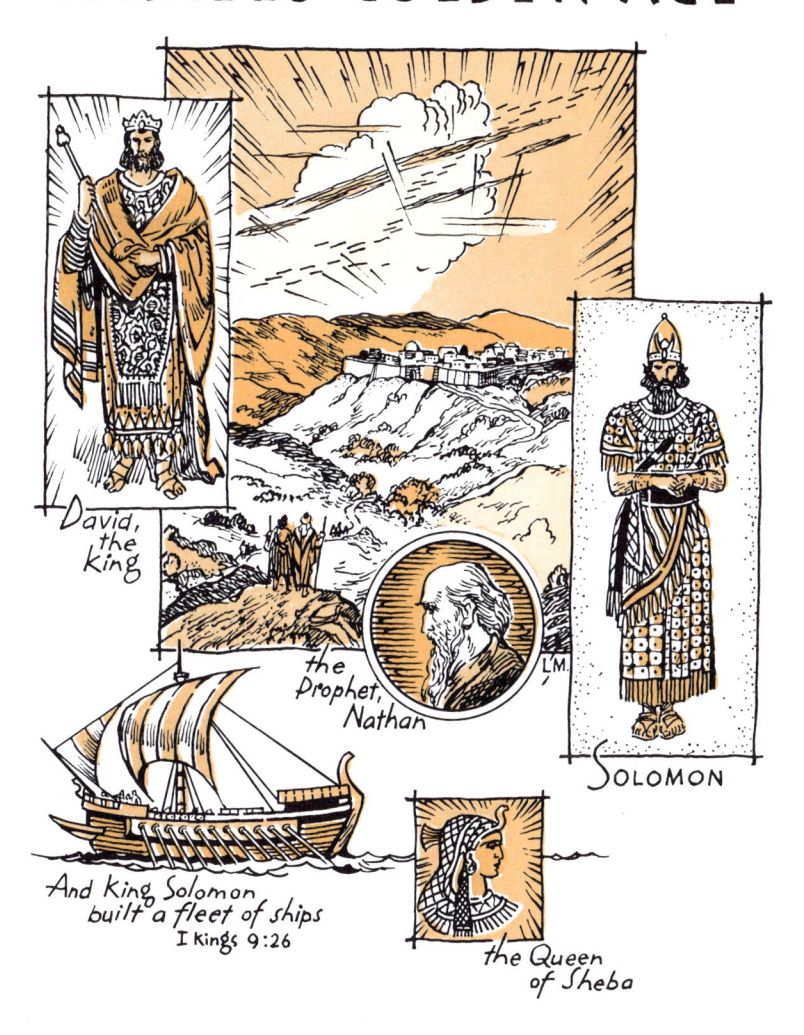

David, the King

the Prophet, Nathan

Solomon

And king Solomon built a fleet of ships
I Kings 9:26

the Queen of Sheba

CHAPTER TWENTY-FIVE

KING DAVID

The Ark is moved to Jerusalem

The first years after Saul's death were violent and chaotic. Then David was implored to take over. He captured the city of Jebus in a daring raid, changed its name to Jerusalem ("City of Peace"), and made it his capital. Then, one after the other, he turned on the Philistines, Moabites, Syrians, Amalekites, and others who made up the ancient ring against Israel, and defeated them. His kingdom now extended from the borders of Egypt to the Euphrates river. They were hard, brutal years, but they were necessary before Israel could have peace. Meanwhile he turned his attention to the establishment of justice and security within the realm. He was so successful that his people enjoyed more stable and prosperous times than they ever before had experienced. David was deeply religious, and it was not long before he moved the ancient Ark of the Covenant from its resting place at Kirjath-Jearim to Mount Zion in Jerusalem. There he reorganized the whole worship set-up, for which he himself wrote a great number of Psalms. He systematized and beautified the service in such a way that he set the pattern for centuries afterward. It was his ambition to replace the old Tabernacle with a more worthy house of God. "I dwell in a house of cedar," he said, "but the Ark of God dwells in a tent." The prophet Nathan also approved of the plan to build it. But when they brought the matter to the Lord, He said no! David had of necessity been a man of war. Such men have not usually been the ones to build houses of religion. It was more fitting that a man of peace do that, the Lord said, and that man would be Solomon, David's son. But he promised David a far greater honor. For in God's own time, a descendant of David would be the Messiah, who would be called the Son of David forever, even Jesus Christ the Redeemer.

David never forgot his debt to the brave men who shared the years of hardship when he was an outlaw fleeing from the wrath of Saul. He rewarded their devotion with positions of trust and referred to them with affection and pride. Twice their names are listed in the Bible as David's heroes, and appended are delightful little stories and anecdotes. One of the most charming and touching chapters in the history of David as king has to do with his treatment of the fallen house of Saul. "Is there still anyone left of the house of Saul, that I may show the kindness of God to him for Jonathan's sake?" he asked. Then they brought to him Saul's grandson, Mephibosheth. When he was small, his nurse had dropped him during the flight after the disastrous battle of Gilboa, and he grew up lame in both feet. David restored to him his father's property and made him a member of the royal household, entitled to eat at the king's table.

It now becomes necessary to record a dark and sordid chapter in David's life, namely his sinful infatuation with Bathsheba, the beautiful wife of Uriah who was one of David's bravest and most trusted soldiers. He committed adultery with her, and then to cover up the consequences, ordered her husband to a post of special danger so as to assure his death in battle.

Thereupon he took Bathsheba to be his wife. God was very displeased and sent the prophet Nathan to him. First Nathan told him a parable that has become famous, of the poor man and his one and only cherished ewe lamb which a rich neighbor took from him to provide a banquet, even though he had large flocks of his own. David was angry and vowed punishment for him. Then Nathan turned to him and said: "Thou art the man!" And he gave him the Lord's message: "I anointed you king over the house of Israel, and I delivered you out of the hand of Saul. And if this were too little, I would add to you much more. Why then have you despised the word of the Lord to do what is evil in his sight? Now therefore, the sword shall never depart from your house." Humbly and tearfully David acknowledged his guilt. Twice he referred to it in Psalms later; and the prophecy came true.

The story of Absalom, David's favorite son, is an illustration. He was conceited and headstrong and caused his father no end of anxiety. Finally he plotted against him for the kingdom, and was so successful that king David fled without so much as offering any resistance. Of course his friends and the nation rallied around him, and the revolt was put down. But to the father the end was just as heartbreaking as the beginning. Absalom was handsome, and particularly proud of his hair, which he let grow very long. This proved his undoing. For after his defeat in battle, when he was fleeing through a forest, his long hair, streaming in the wind, caught in the branches of a tree, the animal he was riding ran away from under him, and he was left hanging in mid-air. After him in hot pursuit came Joab, who slew him with three spears through his body. David was heartbroken when the news came. "O Absalom, my son, my son. Would that I had died instead of you!" he cried. There were also other troubles in his home and in the nation at large, to darken David's old age. Though the sin was forgiven, the scar remained. Nevertheless, David always took his troubles to the Lord, and sang and prayed his way back to peace and reconciliation again. And down through the ages he has remained Israel's Great King, very human but very lovable also, and one of the world's greatest men. II Samuel 3-24 (I Chronicles 10-29)

DAVID MOURNS FOR ABSALOM

CHAPTER TWENTY-SIX

KING SOLOMON

When David was very old and the time came for him to name his successor, he chose Solomon, his son by Bathsheba. Solomon was not only handsome, likeable, and keen minded; but he was devout and a man of peace. One night the Lord appeared to him in a dream and bade him ask for anything he wished. He asked for wisdom to be a good king. And because he had not asked for riches or a long life or the death of his enemies, God granted his prayer; and promised him the other things too, if he would walk in the ways of the Lord.

It was not long before he had a chance to prove his wisdom. Two women came before him with their case. They both lived in the same house, and each had given birth to a child on the same night. Shortly afterward one of the babies died during the night, and its mother went quietly into the room of the other, stole her baby, and placed her own dead child in its place. When the theft was discovered, she claimed the live child as her own and refused to give it up. There were no witnesses, as they were alone in the house at the time. Whose baby should it be? Solomon called for a sword. Then he said: "Divide the living child in two, and give half to one and half to the other." The real mother could not stand this for her little son, and cried out: "O my Lord, give her the living child, and by no means slay it!" But the false mother, who had suffocated her own baby by carelessly lying on it, said: "It shall be neither mine nor yours. Divide it!" Thus Solomon knew by the evidence of mother love who was the true mother, and restored the child to her. This story spread quickly over the whole kingdom, and it was not long before the king became known as Solomon the Wise.

King David had left Israel well united and, generally speaking, in strong and excellent condition. Solomon now set out to make it still stronger, by thoroughly reorganizing the country in all its branches on a better economic and functional basis than it had ever known. He was very energetic and versatile and an excellent leader, and the impact of his wisdom and personality was felt from one end of the country to the other. Never had Israel had such a time of peace and prosperity. Among his many talents, the king also had a feeling for literature and culture. He himself wrote not a little on many subjects and some of his writings are still preserved in our Bible. For instance, the Song of Solomon, which is ascribed to his youth; a large portion of the Book of Proverbs, which is ascribed to his later maturity; and the Book of Ecclesiastes, which is thought by many to have been written by him during his disillusioned old age. Two of the Psalms are also credited to him, according to their headings; and there are two beautiful prayers by him in the Bible. The so-called Wisdom literature of the Old Testament has much of its roots in his day. He brought Israel to the Golden Age of its history, and his fame spread far and wide. Even the Queen of Sheba made a long and dangerous journey to visit and observe this remarkable Hebrew King.

Among the finest things that Solomon did, was to build a Temple of Worship in Jerusalem. David had started the planning of it and had laid aside a huge sum toward its erection, but it was Solomon's privilege to actually build it. Solomon's Temple was not built for size, but for richness and beauty, and was resplendent with gold and ornate furnishings. It was by

building the Temple

far the most beautiful and impressive structure the Israelites had ever known. When it was destroyed many years later, it became their constant dream and struggle to restore it again as it was in Solomon's day. And finally it became the spiritual symbol of the New Testament Temple, "not built with hands," the capital of the Messianic Kingdom.

Solomon continued his building program with a number of other buildings, each more elaborate than the last. He also went in for foreign trade, and Israel was able for the first time in its history to boast that it had a merchant marine and a navy. But as its wealth increased the nation became more and more cosmopolitan, luxuries multiplied together with love of ease and soft living, and both king and people learned to import

The twin pillars of Jachin and Boaz

Supposed form of Solomon's Temple in Jerusalem

Cedars of Lebanon for the Temple

the sins of their foreign neighbors as well as their commodities. As the extravagances of the royal household grew with its court and harem, taxes rose also, higher and higher, until they became a threat and finally an unbearable burden. The Golden Age was slipping into an Age of Gold; religion became more a system of cults and formalism than the Faith of the Fathers; and the country, though outwardly prosperous, was in a bad way. Solomon toward the last was heading his people into bankruptcy and revolt. But God spared the nation until after his death.

In view of all this, it is not easy to give fair and adequate credit to King Solomon for his tremendous achievements. For he did bring Israel to the highest peak in her history, her Golden Age which she never forgot.

I Kings 1-11 (II Chronicles 1-10)

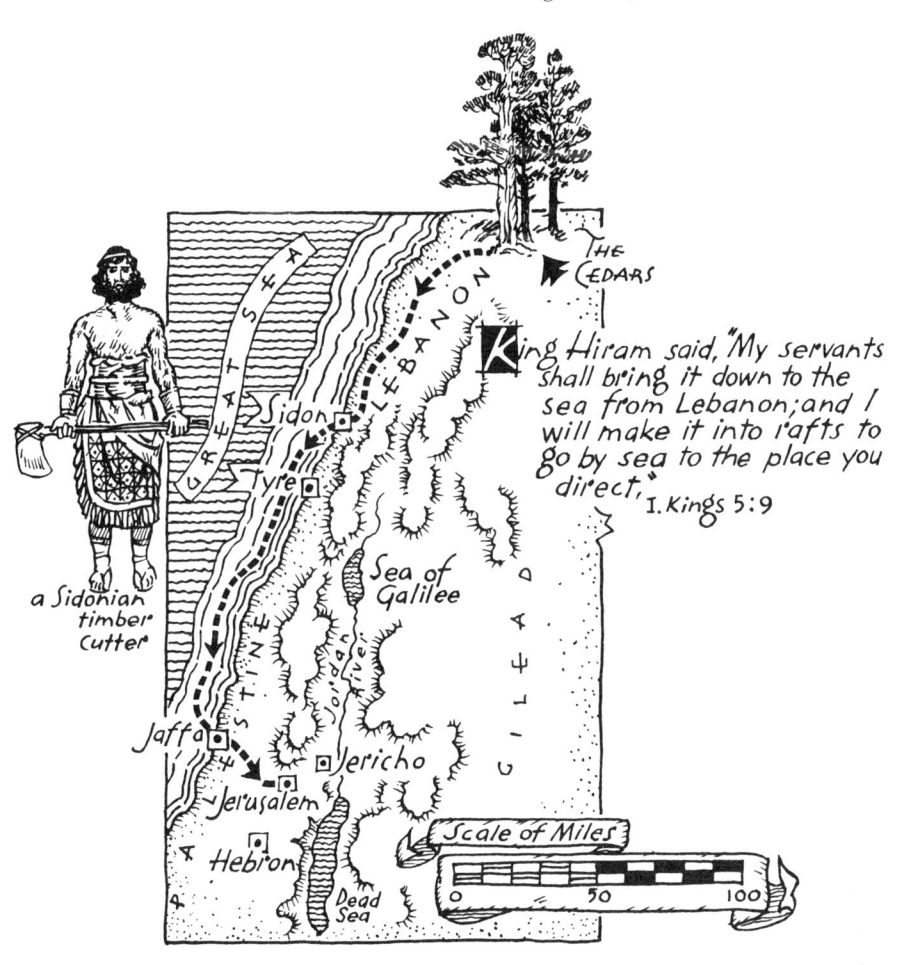

King Hiram said, "My servants shall bring it down to the sea from Lebanon; and I will make it into rafts to go by sea to the place you direct." I. Kings 5:9

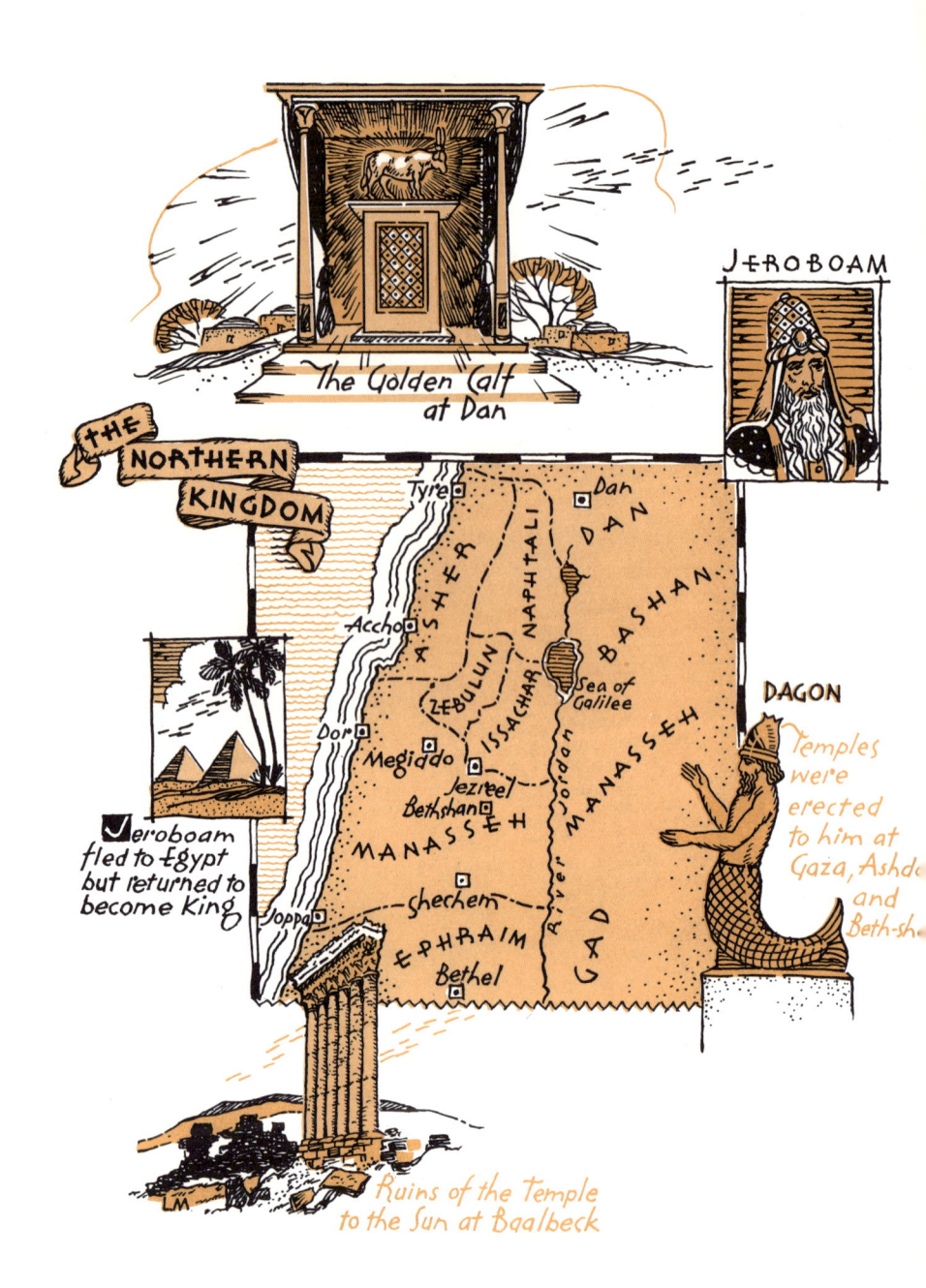

The Golden Calf at Dan

JEROBOAM

THE NORTHERN KINGDOM

Jeroboam fled to Egypt but returned to become King

Tyre
Dan
Accho
ASHER
NAPHTALI
BASHAN
ZEBULUN
ISSACHAR
Sea of Galilee
Dor
Megiddo
Jezreel
Bethshan
MANASSEH
River Jordan
MANASSEH
GAD
Joppa
Shechem
EPHRAIM
Bethel

DAGON
Temples were erected to him at Gaza, Ashdod and Beth-shan

Ruins of the Temple to the Sun at Baalbeck

VIII
A DIVIDED KINGDOM

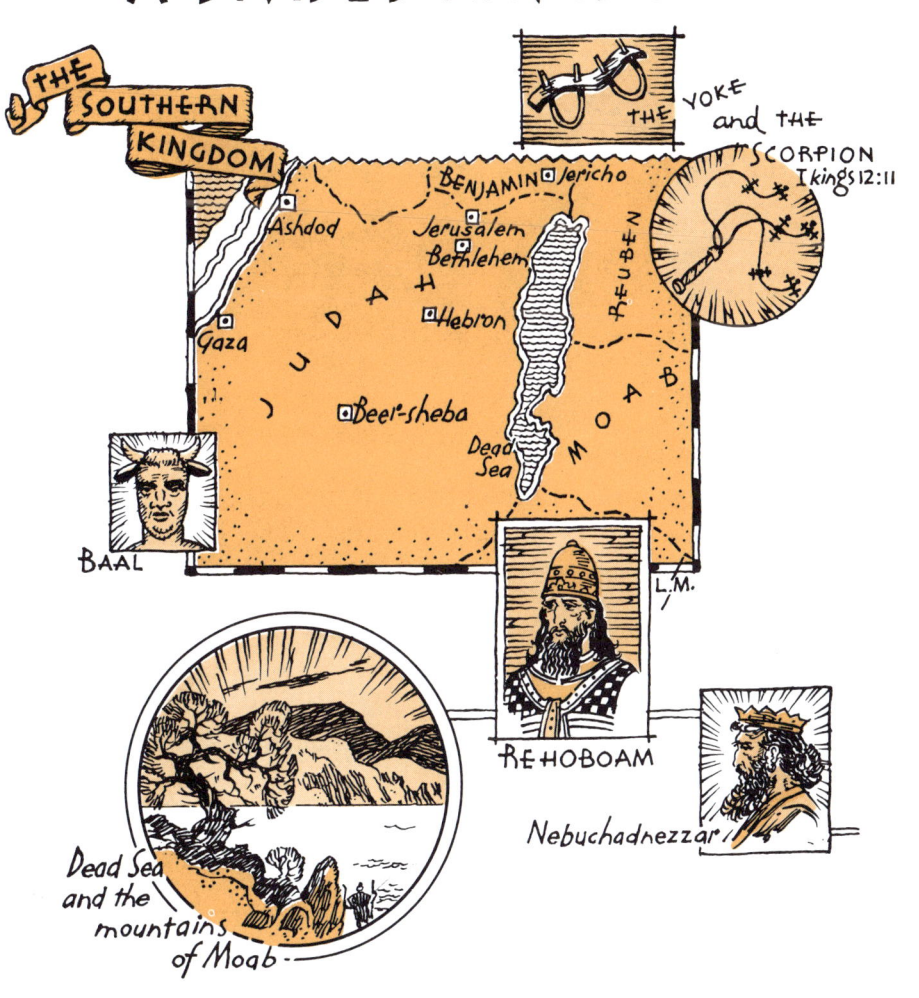

THE SOUTHERN KINGDOM

THE YOKE and the SCORPION
I kings 12:11

BAAL

REHOBOAM

Nebuchadnezzar

Dead Sea and the mountains of Moab

CHAPTER TWENTY-SEVEN

THE KINGDOM DIVIDED

Rehoboam answers the people

When Solomon died, his son Rehoboam became king. He was ill-suited to take over a nation that was ripe for revolt because of high taxes and court extravagances. On his coronation day the people sent a delegation to him asking him to lighten the burdens his father Solomon had placed on them, and promising him allegiance if he would do so. He told them to come back in three days for his answer. Rehoboam refused to take the advice of his older and more level-headed advisers. Instead he listened to the young hotheads and arrogant members of his court. And when the delegation came back he gave them the insolent answer: "My little finger is thicker than my father's loins. My father laid upon you a heavy yoke; I will add to that yoke. My father chastised you with whips; I will chastise you with scorpions." Immediately there was revolt; Rehoboam had ruined his kingdom forever.

He was left with only two tribes, namely Judah and Benjamin, plus a little of other territory. These adopted the name JUDAH, or the Southern Kingdom, with Jerusalem as their capital. The other ten tribes kept the name ISRAEL, and established their capital for a time at Shechem and later at Samaria. Together these tribes formed the Northern Kingdom. The Northern Kingdom chose as its ruler Jeroboam, who had been spokesman for the delegation that brought the petition to Rehoboam regarding taxes. Jeroboam's kingship had been foretold by the prophet Ahijah, and as a result he had had to flee from the wrath of Solomon. He went to Egypt. Now he was back, and became king. Jeroboam could have become an outstanding ruler, for he had a number of things in his favor. He was a talented and clever man; he came in as the leader of a very successful and popular revolution, in a righteous cause; he became king of more than two-thirds of Palestine; and he started with the endorsement of the Lord. But Jeroboam failed to appreciate his opportunity or even to understand his mission as king of God's Chosen People. He had no interest in Israel's spiritual heritage or ideals; indeed he was more of a foreigner than an Israelite, since he had spent much of his time in Egypt. Furthermore he was an evil and a selfish man. One of the first things he did was to set up two golden calves as the center of Israel's religion, one to the north at Dan, and one to the south at Bethel. Their purpose was to draw Israel's thoughts and loyalty away from Jerusalem and the Temple there. It did not take Jeroboam long to lead Israel far on the way back to heathenism and ruin. He was king for about twenty years; his son lasted less than two, and was then murdered; and that was the end of the House of Jeroboam. Baasha, who came next, managed to sit on the throne about twenty-three years, but his son hardly lasted one, and was in turn murdered. And so the pattern went, through nineteen kings and some two hundred years of history. It was one long, bloody period of murders and violence. Not one of Israel's kings was a decent person or attempted to be a servant of the Lord. The Northern Kingdom was finally over-run by Assyria, and destroyed or carried away captive, never to rise again or to be heard of again in sacred history.

The walls of Samaria (from an old print).

In the Southern Kingdom, the pattern was tragic and disgraceful also; but not to the extent of the Northern Kingdom. Rehoboam ruled for about sixteen years. He never gave up the idea of a re-united kingdom, but he had lost his chance forever. Under him, Judah went rapidly down hill, and much of the time was an easy prey to her enemies. But not all of her kings were evil. There were a number of good kings among them, several of whom were outstanding. Judah lasted twice as long as Israel, namely about four hundred years. Finally she, too, was destroyed because of her wickedness, and her inhabitants were either killed or carried away to Babylon. Nevertheless she kept her feeling of national unity, and she did not completely lose her contact with Jehovah God, until toward the very end of her existence as a kingdom. In time her people were permitted to return, and her history as a people went on.

The following is a list of the rulers of Israel and of Judah, together with the years of their reign, as nearly correct as careful scholarship has been able to work it out:—

THE PERIOD OF THE HEBREW KINGS, c. 1000-587 B.C.

THE UNITED MONARCHY
DAVID, c. 1004-998 (as king of Judah)
  c. 998-965 (over all Israel)
SOLOMON, c. 965-926

THE DIVIDED MONARCHY, c. 926-587
(The cross lines mark changes in dynasties)

ISRAEL				JUDAH	
RULER	REIGN	PROPHET	PROPHET	RULER	REIGN
JEROBOAM I	926-907			REHOBOAM	926-910
Nadab	907-906			Abijam	910-908
Baasha	906-883			ASA	908-872
Elah	883-882			JEHOSHAPHAT	
Zimri	882				872-852
OMRI	882-871			Jehoram	
AHAB	871-852			(or Joram)	852-845
Ahaziah	852-851	ELIJAH		Ahaziah	845-844
Jehoram	851-845			Athaliah	845-839
JEHU	845-818	ELISHA		Joash	
Jehoahaz	818-802			(or Jehoash)	839-800
Joash	802-787			Amaziah	800-785
JEROBOAM II	787-747	AMOS		UZZIAH	
Zechariah	747-746			(or Azariah)	785-747
Shallum	747-746	HOSEA		Jotham (regent and king)	758-743
Menahem	746-737		ISAIAH	AHAZ	742-725
Pekahiah	736-735		MICAH	HEZEKIAH	725-697
Pekah	734-733			MANASSEH	696-642
Hoshea	732-724			Amon	641-640
Fall of Samaria	721			JOSIAH	639-609
				Jehoahaz	609
			JEREMIAH	Jehoiakim	608-598
				Jehoiachin	598
			EZEKIEL	Zedekiah	598-587
				Fall of Jerusalem	587

I Kings 12 to II Kings 17

Reprinted from *The Westminster Historical Atlas to the Bible*, edited by George E. Wright and Floyd V. Filson. Copyright 1945, The Westminster Press. Used by permission.

CHAPTER TWENTY-EIGHT

ELIJAH

Bringing offerings to Baal

God continued to call His people with striking and persistent warnings and pleading. He sent earnest, fearless men called prophets to teach and remind them and to be the conscience of the nation. One of the most famous of these was Elijah. His is indeed a dramatic story. Ahab, in the 9th century B.C., was one of the most vile and violent kings that Israel ever had. His wife Jezebel was even worse. Between them they did much to make the horrible worship of Baal the national religion. One day a rough, strange figure crossed Ahab's path. It was the prophet Elijah. Sternly he called the king to account, and ended by prophesying a long period of drought as punishment. Of course Elijah had to flee. He lived near the brook Cherith on the other side of the Jordan, and as the drought grew worse and worse he was fed by ravens that brought food to him. Later he found refuge at the home of a poor widow, right near the place where the king lived. By a miracle Elijah kept up her supply of olive oil and meal, and when her child died he revived it.

Three years after his first meeting with the king, Elijah met him again. Then he challenged the whole priesthood of Baal to a contest on Mount Carmel to prove who was the true God, Jehovah or Baal. On the appointed day a great crowd of people assembled together with hundreds of the heathen priests of Baal. Elijah was alone, but unafraid. The prophets of Baal had first chance. From early morning until past noon they chanted and prayed to their idol; and of course nothing happened. Elijah meanwhile mocked them at the delay and the futility of expecting an answer. "Cry aloud!" he said, "for surely he is a god! Either he is musing, or he has gone aside, or he is on a journey, or perhaps he is asleep and must be awakened." The heathen prophets cried out more loudly and cut themselves with knives, but their god gave them no answer; he was only

Elijah on Mount Carmel

an idol. Now it was Elijah's turn. He prayed confidently and then paused. At that moment God sent lightning from heaven which consumed not only the sacrifice but the wood and the water in the surrounding trench as well. Before long came a cloudburst of rain, the first rain the country had had in three years. The contest on Mount Carmel was a great victory for the true religion, and it stopped the progress of idolatry in Israel for a long time.

a fallen idol

Nevertheless, once more Elijah had to flee, especially from the wrath of Queen Jezebel who hated him more than ever. He fled way down to Mount Horeb, where God had appeared to Moses many centuries before. In his despair for himself and his people, he prayed to die. Then God called him up on the mountain. While he was there a terrific storm took place, but God was not in the storm. It was followed by a terrible earthquake and a fire; but God was not in either one of them. Then there was a great quiet, and Elijah heard a still, small voice; it was God talking to him. He comforted him with the fact that there were still seven thousand in Israel who had not yet bowed the knee to Baal. Then He sent Elijah to anoint Jehu to be king instead of Ahab; and to appoint Elisha to be his own successor as prophet.

Some time after this, king Ahab was busy improving his estate; but he needed more land. The adjoining property belonged to a man named Naboth, but he refused to sell it because it was his homestead. So the king pouted and refused to eat. But Jezebel said: "Let your heart be merry, get up and eat! I will get the vineyard for you!" Then she trumped up a charge against Naboth, accusing him of disloyalty to the government and of blasphemy against God. Poor Naboth was stoned to death and his property taken over by the king, according to the law in such cases. Then the Lord sent Elijah in hot anger to Ahab to say to him: "So you have killed and also taken possession! Thus says the Lord: Where the dogs licked up the blood of Naboth, shall dogs lick up your blood." Some time later, king Ahab was defeated and slain in battle; and when they washed his bloody chariot, the dogs came and licked the blood, just as had been prophesied. Queen Jezebel's death was even more horrible. After defeating Israel thoroughly in battle, Jehu galloped into the capital and up to the palace. There, at his command, the palace servants seized her and threw her down from an upstairs window. The horses trod her under foot and the chariots rolled over her. But when they came to bury her, they could find only scattered fragments of her body; the dogs had done their work. These were years of brutality and terror in the Northern Kingdom. They showed what happens to rulers and people when they embark on careers of violence and crime.

But even at this time God's word was not dead, nor were all the people heathen. There were many who still held on to their sense of decency and remained true to the faith of their fathers.

I Kings 17-21; II Kings 1-2

CHAPTER TWENTY-NINE

ELISHA—END OF THE NORTHERN KINGDOM

The last thing Elijah did before his death was to visit some of the schools of the prophets that still existed in Israel. Elisha went with him. When they reached the Jordan river, Elijah smote the waters and they walked across dry shod just as Joshua had done. Then, as they continued onward, a chariot of fire swooped down upon them and carried the prophet away in a whirlwind. Elisha knew that now his time had come to take over. Tearing his mantle in half as a parting with the past, he threw about him the mantle that Elijah had left behind; and from now on Elisha was God's prophet in his master's place. Many indeed were the wonder-works that he performed. Even the kings were afraid of him, and his fame spread far beyond the land of Israel.

A beautiful illustration of this is the story of Naaman, the captain of the Syrian army. In one of his campaigns he had captured a young Israelite girl who became a trusted servant in his household. Some time later, Naaman was stricken with the dreaded disease, leprosy. His servant girl felt very sorry for him and said to her mistress, "Would that my lord were with the prophet that is in Samaria! He would cure him of the leprosy." This came to the ear of Naaman, and in his distress he decided to visit this famous man, whose name was Elisha. So one day a glittering array of horsemen and chariots drew up before the humble prophet's dwelling. To Naaman's astonishment and exasperation, Elisha did not even come out to greet him. Instead he sent word: "Go and wash in the Jordan seven times and you will be healed." Naaman rode off very angry, saying: "I thought surely that he would come out and at least wave his hand over the place and call on the name of his God. Are not the rivers of Syria better than all the waters of Israel?" But his servants persuaded him to try the prescription anyway, since it was so simple. And he came away

So he went down and dipped himself seven times in the Jordan....
II Kings 5:14

cured. He now tried to reward Elisha with a large gift, but Elisha would not take anything. Naaman was so impressed that he resolved to pray hereafter to Israel's God in preference to his own idols. But Elisha had a servant, Gehazi by name, who was not as highminded as his master. He ran after the Syrian and lied to him, saying that his master had changed his mind about the fee. Elisha had some friends, he said, who needed help, and he would use the fee for them. Very generously Naaman gave the servant far more than he asked, and sent him back. As soon as Gehazi entered the room, Elisha knew what he had done. "Was this a time to accept gifts and money?" he cried. "Therefore the leprosy of Naaman shall cleave to you." And Gehazi went out from his presence a leper, as white as snow.

Many were the stories that gathered around this bold superman of the Old Testament, and his influence for righteousness was felt far beyond his own day. He died just as dramatically as he had lived. Such was the esteem in which he was held that

Israel, 721 B.C.

Assyrian Warriors on the March (from old drawings)

when he was on his deathbed, the king himself came to weep at his bedside. Elisha's last words to him were a prophecy. "Take bow and arrows," he said. "Now open the window to the east and shoot!" and he laid his own hand upon that of the king as he held the bow. The king shot. "It is the arrow of victory over the Syrians," said the dying prophet. "Now take the rest of the arrows and strike the ground with them." The king did so three times and then stopped. "You should have struck more times," cried the prophet, "and you would have defeated Syria permanently! As it is, you shall defeat her only for a while." Later events happened just as Elisha prophesied.

God sent other prophets also to the Northern Kingdom. Among them was Amos, the stern shepherd-prophet from Tekoa. Another was Hosea, with his message of pleading love. But neither one was heeded, and Israel stumbled on to her destruction. In 732 B.C., Assyria conquered Damascus. Her quarrel was with Egypt, but Palestine lay between. Israel bought her off with a huge ransom, but before long she came back. With the Southern Kingdom refusing to help her, Israel did not have a chance! Furthermore the country was so soaked in heathenism and wickedness that there was nothing left to fight for any more, and no spirit with which to fight. The whole country was over-run with terrible destruction and brutality; and such of its people as did not escape to the mountains were either killed or carried away as captives. Israel was no more! As a nation she disappeared from the pages of sacred history and was never heard of again. Assyrian colonists were shipped in to repopulate the country; and they, together with the starving rag and tag of the natives, became a strange mixture of peoples and religions among the weeds and ruins. Such was the tragedy of the Northern Kingdom, that called itself Israel and turned against God. The year was 721 B.C.

I Kings 19; II Kings 2-17

CHAPTER THIRTY

KINGS AND PROPHETS OF JUDAH

War Engine of Uzziah's day

When Rehoboam, the first king of the Southern Kingdom, died, his son Abijam inherited an armed camp of a nation; war was the order of the day, and every male able to carry a weapon was a soldier. Abijam ruled less than three years. He was not the kind of ruler that God could bless. But his son Jehoshaphat was a capable king. He ruled for about a quarter of a century and left memories that earned for him the title of "The Second David." His reforms in state and religion did much for Judah. Toward the last, however, he was not so praiseworthy. After him, the kingdom went down again quickly. It came to an all-time low when a woman took over, the unspeakable Athaliah. She murdered her way to the throne, and was the Jezebel of the Southern Kingdom. Finally the nation could stand her no longer, and she was publicly executed. Then for a short while there was reform again under Joash. Unfortunately, neither did he remain faithful to the end. And so the history of the people went on, up and down, but mostly down.

One of the kings who ruled longest in Judah was Uzziah (also called Azariah in the Bible). He did much to revive the

JOEL — The son of Pethuel

OBADIAH

nation's prestige and strength; he developed a highly trained professional army with military engines and other innovations, and was an outstanding king in many ways. He was also interested in agriculture, and under him the country made great progress economically. But then he too became arrogant and began to quarrel with his God, and the Lord made his star to go down. A new period of luxury and debauchery sent the kingdom to another low that reached bottom under Ahaz. He himself set the pace for his people by burning his own children to the idols of the nation, in the valley of Hinnom near Jerusalem.

But there were many also in the Southern Kingdom who remained faithful to the Lord and who dreamed of and prayed for better kings and better times; nor did God give up His people without many and repeated efforts to win them back. Judah too had her full quota of brave and brilliant prophets, who preached and pleaded in those terrible days. Strange and harsh was the lot of many of them. They had to appeal to people that not only refused to listen but were hostile and even dangerous; and more than one faithful prophet had to suffer imprisonment or lay down his life as a martyr for his message and his Lord. To get a hearing and get at the hearts and consciences of the people, the prophets were often obliged to do strange things as living illustrations of their messages. The record of many of these symbolical acts has been faithfully preserved in the prophetic Books of the Old Testament; and they, too, together with the sermons and prophecies, make up some of the most impressive and interesting of studies.

The most famous of Judah's prophets was Isaiah. He grew up in the capital and was related to the king, but he gave up all and entered the lowly and lonely calling of a prophet. In the midst of wickedness and violence, God gave to Isaiah visions that are among the most amazing and wonderful in the whole Word of God. For instance his vision of the suffering and death of the Messiah are so detailed and accurate that one might think he had stood at the foot of the cross, though the crucifixion took place more than seven centuries later. No wonder he has been called the Gospel Writer of the Old Testament. Among other brave and notable prophets of this period in the Southern Kingdom were Joel, Obadiah, Micah, and Nahum. Writings from their hands are also preserved in the Bible.

Each prophet had a way and a personality all his own. But God gave them all the same central vision. It included the following:—

1. A "Day of Wrath," or time of intense suffering and destruction because of the sins and backslidings of the people.
2. A pleading for repentance, with God's promise of mercy.
3. Warnings to leaders and statesmen that if they left God and righteousness out of their planning, it was useless to depend on foreign alliances and political scheming.
4. The destruction of the kingdom, followed by captivity in a

strange land, but the final return of a "remnant" that would set up the kingdom again.
5. Vision of the coming of the great Messiah some time in the future, who would make all things right between God and man forever. He was given various names, such as "The Anointed One" (the name "Christ" also means the Anointed One), "The Redeemer" ("Goel"), (the name "Jesus" also means the Redeemer or Savior), "The Suffering Servant," "The Son of Man," etc. He would set up a spiritualized Kingdom of David that would have no end.

The message and visions of the prophets, and their fulfilment are among the most amazing and exciting studies in the Bible; and have never been equaled in the literature of any other nation. And the account is told in words of sheerest beauty. II Chronicles 11-28;
The Old Testament Prophetic Books

Mountains of the Old Testament

- **THE ARK** — Gen. 8:4
- **Mt. ARARAT** 17,750 ft
- **THE 10 COMMANDMENTS** — Exodus 20
- **Mt. SINAI** 6,450 ft
- **MOSES VIEWS CANAAN** — Deut. 32:49
- **Mt. NEBO** 2,643 ft
- **THE HOLY CITY** — Psalm 46
- **Mt. ZION** 2,643 ft
- **Mt. HERMON** 9,101 ft — Psalm 89:12
- **The 12 CURSES** — Deut. 27:13-24
- **Mt. EBAL** 2,077 ft
- **CEDARS** — Psalm 29:5
- **Mt. LEBANON** 10,700 ft
- **The 12 BLESSINGS** — Deut. 28:1-14
- **Mt. GERIZIM** 2,849 ft
- **SEA LEVEL**
- **Mt. CARMEL** 1810 ft — I Kings 18:19-40

Mountains have played an important and beautiful part in the story of the Bible, all the way from Mount Sinai to the Mount of Transfiguration, from Ararat to Zion.

ISAIAH wrote (Chap. 52:7) "How beautiful upon the mountains are the feet of him who brings good tidings;"

CHAPTER THIRTY-ONE

END OF THE SOUTHERN KINGDOM

Hezekiah was king over Judah when the Northern Kingdom came to its end. Its destruction was a powerful object lesson to him, and he worked hard to bring his nation back to the Lord. He has come down in history as Hezekiah the Good. But then the Assyrians came on once more under Sennacherib. Terrified, Hezekiah bought them off with a ransom so huge that he had to strip the Temple in order to raise it. Thereupon he tried hard to make a defensive alliance with Egypt. Isaiah warned him against this, but with no success. Before long Assyria was back again thundering at the gates of Jerusalem. In despair, Hezekiah went to the Temple and fell on his face in prayer. "Fear not," Isaiah assured him. "The enemy shall not come into the city nor shoot an arrow there." That night an angel of the Lord swept through the camp of the Assyrians with a contagious pestilence, so terrible and deadly that the survivors fled in a panic. At another time king Hezekiah learned the power of prayer, when he himself became sick unto death and the Lord healed him. On the whole, under Hezekiah

Judah prospered and had good times. But when he died a great change again took place.

His son Manasseh was the opposite of his father, and once more heathenism and brutality were the order of the day. Finally the Lord sent stern words through His prophets that He would punish both king and people most severely and would destroy Jerusalem. In due time, the Assyrians once more appeared before Jerusalem and laid siege. Isaiah was now dead. This time there was no miracle, and Jerusalem was taken. The king himself was captured and carried off to Assyria. But then a miracle did take place. It was nothing less than that Manasseh himself became converted and turned to the Lord. And the Lord permitted him to come back and take over his kingdom again. His last years however, were neither happy nor successful. Manasseh's checkered career as king lasted over half a century, the longest reign that any ruler of Judah ever had. After his death the old pattern set in again, until we come to Josiah his grandson.

JEREMIAH WEEPS

Josiah came in as a boy king only eight years old. But even before he reached young manhood, he showed kingly qualities. In his day the Book of the Law of Moses was re-discovered in the archives of the Temple, and out of it came a spiritual house cleaning that spread to all corners of the kingdom, as the young king strove with heroic efforts to revive his people for God. Then political trouble boiled over again, and once more came war. Josiah was killed in battle with Egypt, and the country which had not entirely appreciated him while he was alive, mourned him with great sorrow when he was dead, recognizing him as one of the greatest kings she had ever had. For a while Egypt controlled Judah, and darkness closed in once more. But it was to be neither Egypt nor Assyria that was to give the death blow to the Southern Kingdom; it was to be Babylon.

The final tragic period of Judah's history also had its group of brave and faithful prophets who pleaded and warned and prayed. For instance, there was Habakkuk, the prophet of justification by faith; and there was Obadiah, the fearless denouncer of Edom; and Zephaniah, the terrible prophet of Judgment Day; and Nahum who prophesied against Nineveh, just as Jonah had done many years before. Meanwhile the Southern Kingdom rushed on to its doom, and neither prophet

AMONG THE RUINS

nor priest nor alliances could save it. It began about 606 B.C., when Nebuchadnezzar burned and looted Jerusalem and carried off many of her inhabitants, including a bright young man named Daniel, of whom we shall learn more later. Some ten years later there was another attack, and among the captives were the king himself and the prophet Ezekiel. Then came another ten years of fear and uneasy existence, and finally the end! Once more Nebuchadnezzar, the Babylonian, appeared before the city walls and laid siege. For a year and a half, Jerusalem held out under unbelievable hardships. Then the enemy broke through and the massacre and destruction began. The city and Temple were completely destroyed, and the starving, helpless people were either killed or led away captive. Jerusalem and her wonderful Temple were no more; the great Babylonian Captivity had begun. Among those who managed to survive was the prophet Jeremiah. For years he had warned his countrymen of this very thing, but they would not listen. Now he sat among the ruins and wept. Then he grasped his pen and drew the picture of what he saw in words of such poetic grandeur that they have been preserved in the Holy Bible ever since as one of the greatest epics of sorrow in existence. This is the book of Lamentations.

II Kings 17-25 (II Chronicles 29-36)

"He has destroyed all its palaces, laid in ruins its strongholds."
Lam. 2:5

OF JERUSALEM

"How lonely sits the city that was full of people!"
Lam. 1:1

IX

EXILE
AND POST-EXILE

CHAPTER THIRTY-TWO

THE BABYLONIAN CAPTIVITY

Daniel interprets the dream

After the first horror was over, the lot of the exiles was not too harsh, except for occasional persecutions. The Jews were settled in colonies here and there and had considerable freedom. Of one such group Daniel became a noted leader, and another was led by Ezekiel. The new life in Babylon's congested districts and cities, commercialized and sophisticated as they were, dazzled many of the younger exiles and their children as they grew up. But for the most part, the Jews were not happy. They longed for the mountains and the lost Temple worship of their fatherland. Jeremiah wrote from Jerusalem and urged them to make the best of things and to wait for the time when they would be permitted to return. The most brilliant prophet of the exile period was Daniel. The king himself recognized his abilities and placed him ahead of all his other advisers, as did also Darius, his successor.

One time king Nebuchadnezzar had a dream. He could not recall it when he woke up, although it haunted him and made him fearful and irritable. None of his wise men could help him, and he finally called in Daniel, who not only described the dream but interpreted it also. The dream had to do with a giant statue. Its head was of burnished gold, its chest and arms of silver, its stomach and thighs of brass, its legs of iron, and its lower feet of clay mixed with the iron. Then a stone "not cut by human hands" smote the statue in its feet and it crashed to the ground and fell apart. But the stone that felled it grew and became so huge that it filled the whole earth. Daniel explained that the giant image represented movements in history. The golden head was Babylon. After it would arise another kingdom not quite so dazzling, of silver. Then one of brass would be succeeded by one of iron mixed with clay. Each of these kingdoms would in turn be destroyed; and then God would set up a Messianic Kingdom that would never be overthrown. Bible scholars still study with amazement Daniel's vision of world history and are pretty well agreed that it was fulfilled as follows:—The Babylonian Empire was succeeded by the Medo-Persian under Cyrus, and this was succeeded in turn by the Greek, under Alexander the Great. Finally came the Roman Empire, hard as iron, but crumbling at its latter end. Then came the great Rock of Ages, which smashed all earthly empires and established the spiritual Messianic Empire of our Lord Jesus Christ, which will last forever.

Nebuchadnezzar had another dream. It grew out of his arrogance as the most powerful ruler of his time. This dream had to do with a huge tree that grew until it towered over the whole earth, so that both man and beast were dependent upon it for food and shelter. Then came a command from heaven that it should be cut down and destroyed, all except the stump which was to be left standing for seven years exposed to wind and weather. The king told his dream to Daniel, who was so horrified when he heard it that he did not want to give the explanation. But the king insisted, and this was its meaning: The great tree was Nebuchadnezzar himself, who because of his arrogance against God would be cut down unless he repented. He would lose his kingship, be driven from the presence of men, and live like a beast of the field until he did repent. Daniel's explanation and pleading with the king were in vain. Not long after, Nebuchadnezzar became insane. He went about on all fours, ate grass, and lived and acted like a beast of the field. Finally, after seven years he came to himself again, repented, and was healed.

His successor to the throne is called Belshazzar in the Bible. He was a cruel monarch and brought about the destruction of the kingdom in his day. It came very suddenly. The king gave a great banquet at which all manner of drunkenness and debauchery took place. Suddenly a hand was seen, writing on the wall opposite the king. "Mene, mene, tekel upharsin" it wrote in Chaldaic characters from right to left. Terrified, the king sent for Daniel, who interpreted the writing. "Numbered, numbered, weighed and divisions" it said: "Numbered, numbered art thou; weighed in the balances and found wanting!" That very night the Medes and Persians broke in upon them, Belshazzar was slain, and the Babylonian empire was no more.

Another great prophet of the exile was Ezekiel. His visions had to do with the return from captivity and the rebuilding of the temple. But Daniel and his friends had other experiences too that were not pleasant. At one time when they refused to bow down to a huge idol that Nebuchadnezzar had erected of himself, they were thrown into a fiery furnace. But they were saved by a miracle, and the king was so impressed that he restored them to their places of honor again. Another time when Darius was king, he had Daniel thrown into a den of lions for refusing to bow down and worship the king. Again the Lord kept him unharmed, and the king restored him to his former position. Because of his virtuous life, his many talents and courage, and his great trust in the Lord, Daniel has been called the Second Joseph of the Old Testament.

The Book of Daniel; the Book of Ezekiel

CHAPTER THIRTY-THREE

END OF THE BABYLONIAN CAPTIVITY

The return to the ruined city

Another notable incident from this time is the story of Queen Esther. When Ahasuerus was ruler of the Persian empire, he gave a huge and lavish banquet at which many wicked things took place. When his wife, Queen Vashti, refused to display herself before his drunken revellers, he deposed her. Then a search was made for the most beautiful girl in the land to become queen in her stead. The choice fell upon a Jewish girl named Hadassah. She was an orphan living with her foster-father Mordecai, a devout as well as talented man. The king fell very much in love with Hadassah, changed her name to Esther, which means a star (Hadassah means a myrtle). But to be his queen was a dangerous honor; for she was a member of a down-trodden race, her master was a fickle oriental king, and she was surrounded by jealous courtiers and scheming enemies. The story of how Esther, with her wisdom and her beauty, won the respect as well as the love of the king, how she and Mordecai foiled a plot against the king's life, and how she used her womanly charms to prevent a massacre of the Jews, makes one of the most stirring epics in the Old Testament.

Another story that may have originated about this time is that of Job, though he seems to have actually lived way back in the days of the Judges. Job, a righteous and God-fearing man, became afflicted with sickness and other terrible calamities, and so the question arose: why do righteous people have to suffer, if suffering is God's punishment for sin? The answer in the Book of Job is that while the Almighty is not accountable to man for His actions, a righteous man can suffer and at the same time be in favor with God, and that such visitations are often God's chastening process and His test of His children's faith.

The years of the Babylonian Captivity came to a close when the Medo-Persians conquered Babylon and Cyrus the Great took over. Cyrus was a remarkable man in many ways, and his brilliant and rapid conquests soon made him master of a considerable portion of the ancient world. He was very sympathetic toward the Jews and gave as many of them as wanted it permission to return to their fatherland. Not all did so. Many of them had so thoroughly lived themselves into their new surroundings that they did not care to face the hardships of returning. The first company that went back consisted of about forty-five thousand under the leadership of Zerubbabel.

When they arrived they found ruins and desolation. Yet they were so happy, the Bible tells us, that they sang and laughed for joy. They immediately set to work rebuilding the Temple. But there were many difficulties. The Samaritans, who had escaped the Babylonian captivity and were now natives of the place, asked to be along in the rebuilding but were refused. From then on they were the enemies of the Jews and did everything they could to hinder the work. The next thing was crop failure, with poverty and suffering. Gradually the Temple work slowed up and finally stopped for a time. Tirelessly the prophets Haggai and Zechariah urged the people on, alternately comforting and scolding them. They also gave them visions of the final Messianic Temple that would come about some day and remain forever. Finally the House of God was completed about twenty years after the cornerstone had been laid. To those that could still remember the old Temple of Solomon, it was a disappointment, and the shouts of joy were intermingled with voices of weeping.

About sixty years after the first home-coming, another company of about fifteen hundred arrived under the leadership of Ezra. It brought generous supplies and new ambition; and these were badly needed as life among the earlier settlers was at a low ebb. Ezra, with authority from the king, immediately started drastic reforms. He began with the mixed marriages and low morals in family life. But the task was difficult, and it took both courage and time. A number of years later, a third company under Nehemiah arrived from Babylon. It was now almost a century since the first group had arrived, but the colony was still far from being settled or secure. Zerubbabel's lot had been to rebuild the temple; Ezra's calling was that of a reformer; now it was to be Nehemiah's task to rebuild the walls of Jerusalem and establish security and unity there. He and Ezra made an excellent team. The reforms that Ezra had begun were now pushed harder than ever. The rebuilding of the city walls was conducted under the greatest dangers and difficulties because of the enmity of the Samaritans. Indeed there were times when the workers had to take turns standing guard, with weapons in their hands, while others worked. But the work went on at full pace. In fifty-two days during the hottest part of the summer, the work was completed. "So we built the wall," Nehemiah wrote with pride afterward, "for the people had a mind to work."

The work of these three heroes, Zerubbabel, Ezra, and Nehemiah, saved the colony and possibly the whole land of the Jews from extinction. Now at last their people could work and sleep in safety and be united once more. Thus, with tears and with joy, God's people returned from the Babylonian Captivity.   The Books of Esther, Job, Ezra and Nehemiah

CHAPTER THIRTY-FOUR

THE MACCABEES

Cleansing the Temple

The rebuilding of the Temple by Zerubbabel united the Jews as to their religion again; the reforms under Ezra unified them as a nation; and the rebuilding of the walls of the capital city under Nehemiah gave them new security against the outside world. Thus for the next two centuries, Palestine had comparative peace. Local government was under the High Priest, assisted by a Council of Elders which finally became the Sanhedrin of Jesus' day. The position of high priest became a powerful and coveted one, and more and more worldly; and as time went on there was much scheming, scandal, and bloodshed connected with it.

In 335 B.C., in Greece a young man barely twenty years old took over the kingdom of his murdered father, Philip of Macedon. His name was Alexander, which he soon turned into Alexander the Great. Within a decade he had conquered the rest of Greece, spilled over into Asia Minor, including Syria, Palestine, and Egypt, and annexed as much of interior Asia, including India, as his weary legions cared to bother with. Three years later he filled a drunkard's grave; he had conquered everyone except himself! And yet, perhaps no man in secular history has so profoundly affected the life of western mankind as Alexander did. For wherever he went he planted Greek colonies and culture which have influenced western civilization, in spite of the interruption of the Middle Ages, way down to our own day.

It was fortunate for the Jews that they found favor with this temperamental monarch. For he spared their capital, respected their religion, and gave them a long breathing spell in history. Moreover God willed that Greece was to play an important part in preparing the world for the Messiah by laying the way of an international language, culture, and sense of beauty.

Unfortunately, when Alexander died his empire fell apart, each of his four generals wrestling for a piece. Palestine and Egypt fell to Ptolemy Lagi with the capital at Alexandria in Egypt; while Syria and Babylon and the land east of the Jordan were taken over by Seleucus with Antioch in Syria as the capital. Between Syria and Egypt there was continual enmity. Nevertheless, for about a century Palestine fared pretty well.

About 200 B.C., a beast by the name of Antiochus III got the upper hand over Syria. He then seized Palestine, and the

The High Priest in Robes

next generation saw the worst persecutions that Israel had ever known. It became the ambition of the Syrians to stamp out every vestige of Jewish lore and religion, and force upon the Jews the gods and ways of paganism. Never had the spiritual heritage of the Chosen People been in greater danger. The climax came about 175 B.C., under Antiochus Epiphanes. He laid waste the greater part of Jerusalem, and stripped the Temple of everything that had any value. Then a statue of the Greek god Zeus was erected atop the Great Altar of burnt offerings, and every manner of insult was directed against the Jews and their religion. Their sacred Scriptures were ordered destroyed; religious festivals, including the Sabbath, were abolished, and Epiphanes himself entered the Holy of Holies, sacrificed swine on the Altar of Burnt Offerings, and as a final touch sprinkled broth made of swine's flesh all over the place.

At this time there was living northwest of Jerusalem a devout priest by the name of Mattathias. He both raged and wept as he watched what was going on. One day he noticed one of his own countrymen offering heathen sacrifices together with a Syrian officer. In a rage he slew them both and tore down the altar. Then, like Moses, he had to flee, and with him went his five brave sons, together with a group of other patriots. Like

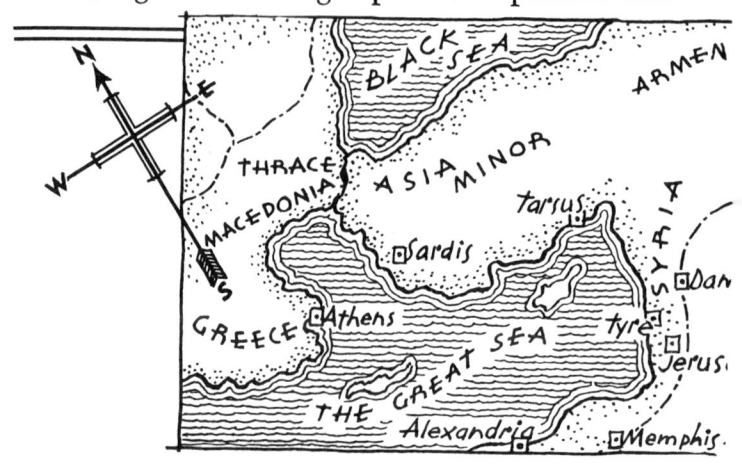

David in the "hold" when Saul pursued him, Mattathias soon had a hardened though ragged little army around him that became a scourge and a terror to the enemy. But Mattathias was now old and soon after this he died. His son, Judas Maccabaeus, succeeded him (166 B.C.) and has come down in history as one of the bravest champions in the history of religion. These patriots took the name of "Maccabees" from the initials of the Hebrew words in Exodus 15:11; and they made their symbol a hammer, from the Hebrew word formed by the same letters. And a hammer they proved to be. Antiochus himself was defeated, the temple was cleansed, and the old time religion was set up again. Then an alliance was made with Rome, but alas! her help never came. The Syrians meanwhile rallied, and Judas Maccabaeus fell in a disastrous battle in 161 B.C.

His brother Jonathan continued the unequal struggle. In 143 B.C., the Syrians deceived him into attending a parley, imprisoned him and finally murdered him. A third brave brother, Simon, now took over. He and his two sons were slain by the treachery of his own son-in-law. But his third son, John Hercanus, forced the Syrians to make peace, and finally brought the years of agony to an end. The period of the Maccabees lasted from about 165 to 63 B.C. It was a century of heroes!

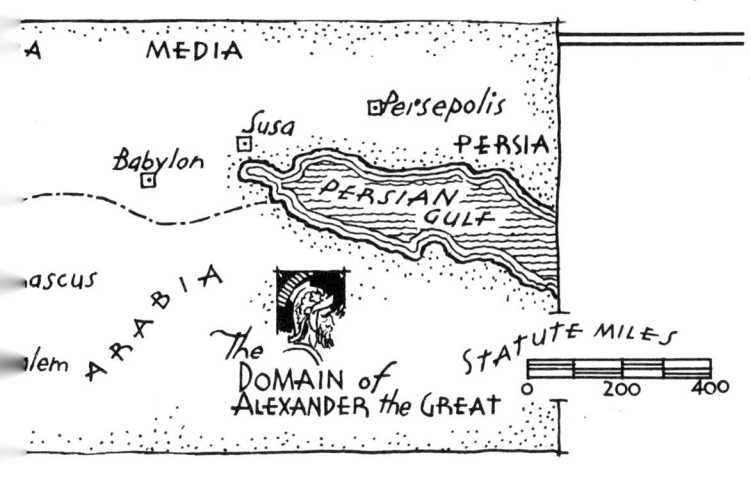

CHAPTER THIRTY-FIVE

END OF THE OLD TESTAMENT

The Old Testament record of our Bibles ceases about 450 or 400 B.C. with the book of Malachi. By this time the exiles had returned from Babylon, the Temple and city walls had been rebuilt, and enough time had gone by for the people to settle down after all the excitement, and show their old traits of carelessness and sinfulness again. The Book of Malachi is therefore a book of warnings to both priests and people. It closes with a Messianic prophecy, the last in the Old Testament: "Behold I will send you Elijah the prophet, before the great and terrible day of the Lord comes. And he will turn the hearts of fathers to their children and the children to their fathers, lest I come and smite the land with a curse." So the long line of Old Testament prophets came to an end, and Holy Scripture fades into a silent wait of almost half a thousand years until the "fulness of time" when the Savior should come.

The list of these prophets is a roll call of heroes that should be studied earnestly. Here they are (the dates of their service are only estimates):—

Elijah	875-850 B.C.
Elisha	850-800
Joel	840-830 (?)
Jonah	790-770 (?)
Amos	780-740
Hosea	760-720
Isaiah	750-695
Micah	740-700

    End of Northern Kingdom 721 B.C.

Zephaniah	640-608
Nahum	630-608 (?)
Jeremiah	625-586
Habakkuk	606-586
Obadiah	586-(?)
Daniel	606-534
Ezekiel	592-570

    End of Southern Kingdom 587 B.C.

    First group returns from captivity 536 B.C.

Haggai	520-516
Zechariah	520-516

    Completion of the Temple 516 B.C.

Malachi	450-(?)

Writers and prophets of a less exalted degree continued to appear however, and a whole treasury of literature sprang up. These writings were never considered a part of inspired Holy Writ. The older printed Bibles used to include about fourteen of them as a sort of supplement to the Old Testament. They are known as the "Apocrypha" or "hidden writings." It does not take the reader long to discover their inferiority to inspired Scripture. But occasionally they do contain passages of rare beauty and devotion, and they give interesting side-lights to the Bible student on the period of history just preceding the

New Testament. They also contain many references to the coming of the Messiah and are an indication that the great Promise was not forgotten and that the people longed and prayed for His coming. In view of the terrible persecutions that the Jewish people went through during those years, it is understandable that they had a tendency to picture the Messiah as a military genius and political leader who would avenge His people against their enemies and set up an earthly kingdom by force. The tragedy of their error was that it led them to refuse to recognize Him when He did come, and they closed their hearts to His proclamation that His kingdom was far greater and more wonderful than any earthly kingdom—it was a spiritual kingdom of love and forgiveness that would embrace the whole world and carry over into eternity.

The Apocryphal books of the Old Testament have a certain value however. For instance, not a little of the information and data concerning the years when Palestine was under the power of the Greeks and when the Maccabees struggled against the enemy, comes from these books, particularly the Books of the Maccabees. They also include a number of clever sayings and observations, not unlike the Book of Proverbs or Ecclesiastes, and other examples of exalted and noble thinking. But, as intimated, they are full of errors, superstition, and absurdities, and contain unworthy and even wrong conceptions and ideas. It is no wonder that they were not admitted as a part of inspired Scripture.

Another type of literature that sprang up during those "in-between" centuries, between the Old and New Testaments, is known as the "Pseudepigrapha," or "false" or "pretended" writings. They are more preposterous and impossible than even the worst of the Apocrypha. They were lost for many centuries and have been re-discovered and translated in modern times. The most notable of these is doubtless the book of Enoch, and there is some evidence that New Testament writers were familiar with it, for instance Paul in II Cor. 12:2. The so-called Odes or Hymns of Solomon (not the Old Testament

King Solomon), were discovered and translated as late as 1909 by Dr. Rendel Harris. The writings of the Pseudepigrapha came late and carried over into the Christian era. The more one reads these ancient writings, the more the superiority of the recognized canon of our Holy Bible becomes clear; and we begin to realize the guidance and inspiration that the Lord gave to those who wrote it, and to those who so carefully sifted and eliminated all false and unreliable writings and established and preserved the Bible in its final form once and forever. It is a treasure that we cannot value too highly!

Ancient Scrolls and Seals

CHAPTER THIRTY-SIX

ROME AND THE FULLNESS OF TIME

the City of Seven Hills

After the long, brave struggle of the Jews to obtain their freedom, it is disheartening to note that the successors of John Hercanus were unable to behave themselves and keep peace with each other, and so round out the "century of heroes" mentioned in our last chapter. It came to a climax with two brothers fighting one another for the throne. Neither of them being able to win, each called on Rome to come to his aid. Pompey was not far away with his legions; and he came in true Roman style and according to the old familiar pattern. Having taken Jerusalem, he sacked and massacred and burned in all directions, and then looted the Temple. Thereupon he set up one of the contending brothers as ethnarch under Syria, and made the whole setup a vassal of Rome, and departed.

Rome was the latest contender for Queen of the Universe, and she was doing mighty well. She had a brilliant history behind her as a republic, but had lately been on a decline. Now she was on the way upward toward becoming an empire under a dictating emperor. As might be expected, that way was greased with blood, and that, too, of some of the greatest men in history. The transition was not yet complete. Two rival generals were fighting it out, namely Gnaeus Pompey and Julius Caesar. Of the two, Caesar was the greater man, but Pompey got the earlier start. His Asiatic campaign, which took in Palestine, pushed Rome's frontiers as far east as the Euphrates River, and he came home as Pompey the Great. In his triumphal procession marched three hundred and twenty-four captive princes, while inscribed on banners was the legend that he had conquered twenty kings, subjugated twelve million people, and doubled the revenues of the state. But Pompey's glory was short-lived, for he was defeated in battle by Julius Caesar and fled to Egypt, where he was murdered. In 44 B.C. Caesar was stabbed to death. And that was that. It of course meant some readjustments in the four districts that included Palestine.

So it happened that about 40 B.C. the unspeakable Herod, styled The Great, became supreme ruler of that little corner of the globe where the King of Glory, our Lord Jesus Christ, was to be born. Meanwhile Herod made an immediate bid to greatness by murdering the rest of the Maccabaean family, on the supposition that they might stand in his way. Then he went on a spending and building spree that included everything from sea ports and public baths, to sewers, aqueducts, theaters, palaces, and even the Temple itself. Zerubbabel's venerable House of God was by now half a thousand years old, and was battle-scarred and shabby. So Herod decided to rebuild it on a scale more commensurate with himself. He did not live to see the building completed. But that did not matter a great deal; because in a sort of cave only about six miles south of his proud capital, a little infant was soon to be born who would push out of existence Herod and his buildings, his tinseled, bloody greatness and his very kingdom itself. For we have come to the Fullness of Time.

At the time our Lord was born, it was a pretty compact world that had been prepared for His coming. In the first place, it was under one central government, to an extent that has never been known either before or since. In spite of rotten politics and the immensity of such an empire, this meant at least comparative peace and security. In the second place it meant highways and regular intercourse between country and country, and community and community. In the third place it meant regular and recognized processes under common law. Two international languages were in universal use at that time. The Latin was the language of court and business. The Greek was the language of culture and literature and philosophy. And for God's children of those days, Hebrew was also an international language, the language of religion and revelation. All these things made for rapid and effective spreading of the Gospel when the proper time came.

Meanwhile, the old conceptions and ideas in religion and morality were outworn and ready to be discarded. The way of sacrifice as a way of worship, with its bloody altars and incantations was outlived; and the self-centered attitude of priests, and their inability to help the people and make the world happier or better, or to give dying souls assurance before God were becoming more and more evident. Underneath it all was a universal feeling of spiritual despair, and a restless longing for something better. Thus in a negative and in a positive way, God was preparing the world for the coming of Christ. But the Old Way died hard and the New Way had to have its brave martyrs first, before even a Gospel of love and forgiveness and eternal happiness could break through.

Thus it was in the days when our Lord came into the world.

OUR LORD WAS BORN

INDEX

Aaron, 73, 79 f., 93
Abel, 21 f.
Abijam, 145
Abishai, 115
Abner, 112
Abraham (Abram), 32 ff., 36 ff., 39 ff.
Absalom, 122 f.
Adam, 16 f., 19 ff.
Ahab, 136 ff.
Ahasuerus, 160
Ahijah, prophet, 133
Alexander the Great, 164 ff.
Alexandria (Egypt), 165
Amalekites, 79, 110, 120
Ammonites, 109
Amorites, 87, 97
Amos, prophet, 143
Antioch, 165
Antiochud III, 165 f.
Antiochus Epiphanes, 166
Apocrypha, 169 f.
Arabs, 35
Ark of the Covenant, 90 f., 106, 120 f.
Ark of Noah, 23 f.
Asia Minor, 164
Assyria, 28, 133, 143 f., 150 ff.
Athaliah, 145
Azariah (Uzziah), 145

Baal, 136 ff.
Baal-Peor, 87
Baasha, 133
Babylonia, 28, 134, 152 f., 156 ff., 168
Babylonian Captivity, 153, 156 ff., 160 ff.
Balaam, 87
Balak, 87
Barak, 97
Bashan, 87
Bathsheba, 121, 124
Belshazzar, 158
Benjamin, son of Jacob, 54, 63 ff.

Benjamin, tribe, 107, 132
Bethel, 32, 47, 133
Bethlehem-Judah, 100, 102, 173
Beth-shan, 116
Bethuel, 43
Birthright, 44 ff.
Boaz, 102
Burning Bush, 73

Cain, 21 f.
Caleb, 84
Canaan, 86 f., 89 ff.
Carmel, Mt., 137 f.
Chariot of Fire (Elijah), 140
Cherith, 136
Commandments, 82 ff., 92
Creation, 14 ff.
Cyrus, 157, 161

Damascus, 33, 143
Dan, tribe, 133
Daniel, prophet, 153, 156 ff.
Darius, 156, 159
David, 112 f., 114 ff., 120 ff., 124 f.
Day of Atonement, 90
Day of Wrath, 147, 152
Dead Sea, 8
Dead Sea Scrolls, 9
Deborah, 97
Delilah, 99
Dreams, 47, 54, 59 ff., 157 f.

Eden, 17, 19 f.
Edom, 86, 152
Egypt, 32, 56, 59 ff., 63 ff., 68 ff., 73 ff., 77 ff., 120, 143, 150, 152, 164, 173
Eli, 105 f.
Eliezer, 41 f.
Elijah, prophet, 136 ff., 140 ff.
Elisha, prophet, 140 ff.
Elkanah, 105
Endor, witch of, 116

177

Enoch, 22; Book of, 170
Ephraim, son of Joseph, 61
Ephraim, the place, 93
Esau, 44 ff., 47 ff., 86
Esther, 160 f.
Euphrates, 120, 173
Eve, 17, 19 f.
Ezekiel, prophet, 153, 156, 159
Ezra, 162, 164

Fall of Man, 19 f.
Flood, 23 f.
"Fulness of Time," 172 ff.

Galilee, Sea of, 9, 32
Gehazi, 142
Gideon, 96 f.
Gilboa, 116, 121
Gilgal, 92
Goel (Redeemer), 148
Golden Age, 126, 128
Golden Calf, 80, 133
Goliath, 111
Gomorrah, 33, 36 f.
Goshen, 66, 68 ff., 74
Greece, 157, 164, 174

Habakkuk, prophet, 152
Hadassah (Esther), 160 f.
Hagar, 34
Haggai, prophet, 162
Hannah, 105
Harris, Dr. Rendel, 171
Hebrew Language, 174
Hebron, 33
Hercanus John, 167
Herod the Great, 173
Hezekiah, 150 f.
Holy Land, 7 ff., 32 ff.
"Holy of Holies," 90
"Holy Place," 90
Horeb, 78, 138
Hosea, prophet, 143
Hur, 79

India, 164
Isaac, 38, 39 ff., 44 f.
Isaiah, prophet, 147, 150 f.
Ishmael, 34 f.
Israel, tribes of, 93, 132 f., 139, 140 ff.

Jacob, 44 ff., 47 ff., 54 ff., 63 ff., 68
Jebus, 120
Jehoshaphat, 145
Jehu, 139
Jephthah, 97
Jeremiah, prophet, 153, 156
Jericho, 89 ff.
Jeroboam, 133
Jerusalem, 9, 120, 151, 153, 166, 172
Jesse, 104, 112
Jesus Christ, 34, 41, 76, 86 ff., 121, 157, 173 f.
Jethro (Reul), 71, 79
Jezebel, 136 ff.
Joash, 145
Job, 161
Joel, prophet, 147
Jonah, prophet 152
Jonathan, 109 f., 114, 116, 121
Jonathan (Maccabee), 167
Jordan River, 8, 92
Joseph, 54 ff., 59 ff., 63 ff., 93
Joshua, 84, 89 ff.
Josiah, 151 f.
Judah, 56, 64 f., 132, 134 f., 145 ff., 150 ff.
Judas Maccabaeus, 167
Judges, 96 ff.
Julius Caesar, 173
Justification by Faith, 152

Kadesh-Barnea, 84
Kirjath-Jearim, 120
Kish, 107
Korah, 84

Laban, 43, 48
Languages of the Bible, 4, 174

178

Laws of Moses, 82 ff., 92
Leah, 48
Lot, 32, 27

Maccabees, 164 ff., 167, 170, 173
Macedonia, 157, 164, 174
Malachi, prophet, 169
Manasseh, 61; tribe of, 87; King, 151
Manna, 78, 86
Mattathias, 166 f.
Medo-Persian, 157 f., 161
Melchizedek, 33
"Mene, mene, tekel, upharsin," 158
Merchant Marine, Israel, 127
Messianic Prophecies and references, 20, 34, 41, 76, 86 ff., 121, 127, 147 f., 157, 165, 168 ff., 173 f.
Methuselah, 22
Micah, prophet, 147
Midianites, 70 f., 87, 96 f.
Miriam, 69, 78
Moabites, 87 f., 100, 120
Mordecai, 160 f.
Moriah, Mt., 38
Moses, 68 ff., 73 ff., 77 ff., 82 ff., 86 ff.

Naaman, 140 ff.
Naboth, 139
Nahor, 41
Nahum, prophet, 147, 152
Naomi, 100 ff.
Nathan, 122
Nazarite, 97
Nebuchadnezzar, 153, 156 ff.
Nehemiah, 162 f.
New Jerusalem, 9
Nile, 56
Nineveh, 152
Northern Kingdom (Israel), 132 f., 139, 140 ff.; List of Kings, 135

Obadiah, prophet, 147, 152
Obed, 103
Og, 87
Original Sin, 20 ff.
Orpah, 100

Palestine, 7 ff., 32 ff., 164 f.
Paradise, 17, 19 f.
Passover, 75 f.
Pharaoh, 56, 59 ff., 63 ff., 68 ff., 73 ff., 78 ff.
Philip of Macedon, 164
Philistines, 97 ff., 106, 109 ff., 116, 120
Pisgah, Mt., 88
Plagues of Egypt, 74 ff.
Polygamy, 22, 34 f., 44 ff., 47, 54, 121 f.
Pompey, 172 f.
Prophets, 136, 146 f., 152; List of, 169
Pseudepigrapha, 170 f.
Ptolemy Lagi, 165
Pyramids, 56

Rachel, 48, 54
Rahab, 89 f.
Rebekah, 42 f.
Red Sea, 77 ff.
Rehoboam, 132, 134
Reuben, 56; Tribe of, 87
Reuel (Jethro), 71, 79
Roman Empire, 157, 167, 172 ff.
Ruth, 100 ff.

Sabbath, 16
Sacrifices, 38 f., 175
Samaritans, 133, 161 f.
Samson, 97 ff.
Samuel, 105 ff., 110, 114 ff.
Sanhedrin, 164
Sarah (Sarai), 32 ff., 36 ff., 41
Satan, 19 f.
Saul, 107 f., 109 ff., 114 ff., 120 f.
Seleucus, 165
Sennacherib, 150
Serpent, 19 f., 86
Seth, 22
Sheba, Queen of, 126
Shechem, 32, 133
Simeon, 63 f.
Simon (Maccabee), 167
Sinai, Mt., 78 ff., 82 ff.

Sodom, 33, 36 f.
Solomon, 121 f., 124 ff., 132
Solomon, Odes of, 170
"Son of Man," 148
Southern Kingdom (Judah), 132, 134 f., 145 ff., 150 ff.; Kings of, 135
Star of Jacob, 87
"Still small voice," 139
"Suffering Servant," 148
Syrians, 120, 165 f., 172

Tabernacle, 90 f., 121
Tekoa, 143
Temple, Solomon's, 121, 126 ff., 133, 153; Herod's, 173; Zerubbabel's, 161 ff., 164, 166, 172 f.
Terah, 32
Tithing, 34

Tree of Knowledge, 19
Tree of Life, 19

Uriah, 121
Uzziah (Azariah), 145

Vashti, Queen, 160

Wondering of the Israelites, 84 f., 86 ff.
Wisdom Literature, 126
Wrestling of Jacob, 49

Zechariah, prophet, 169
Zephaniah, prophet, 152
Zerubbabel, 161, 164
Zion, Mt., 120
Zipporah, 71

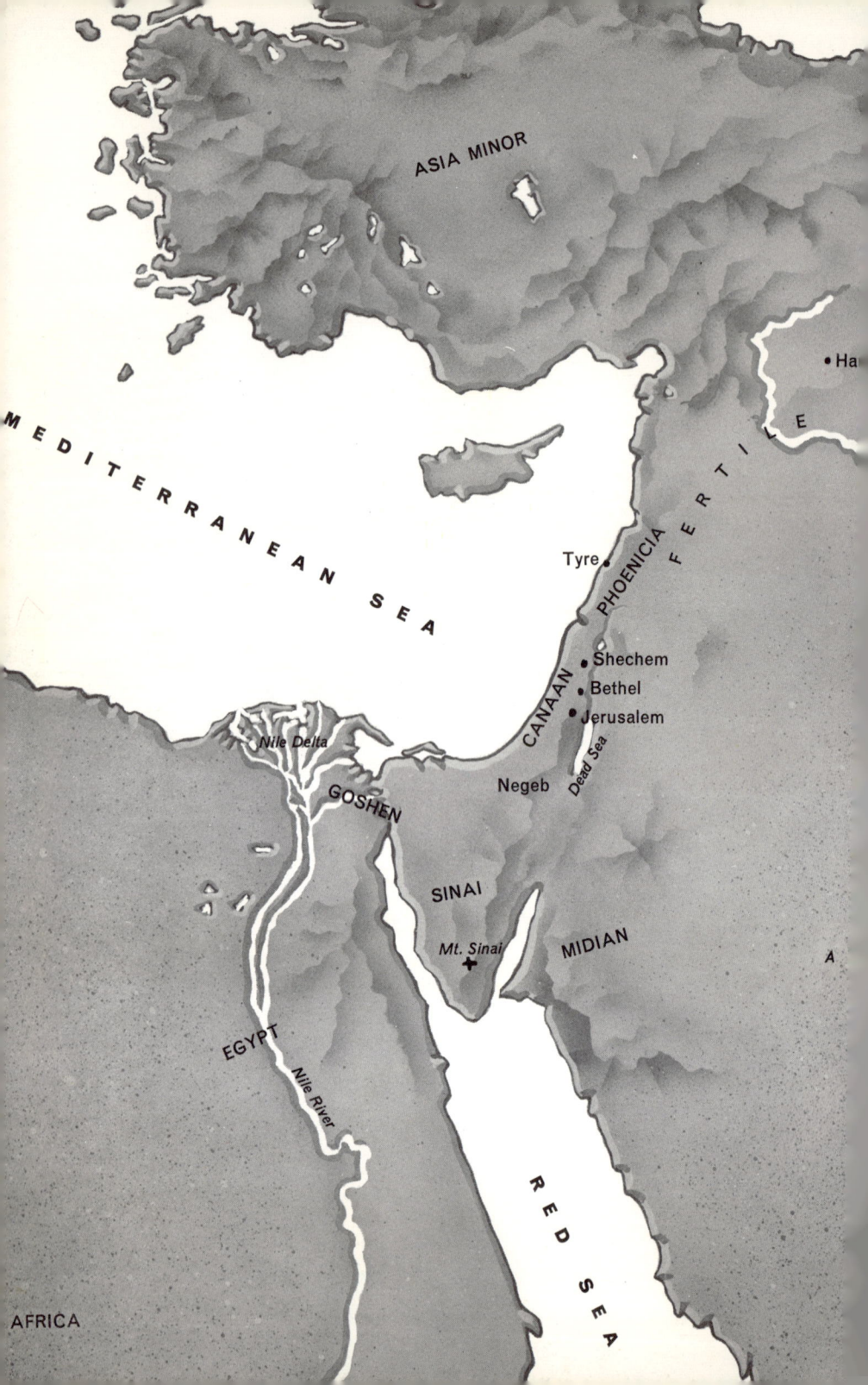